Embodied

A self-care guide for sensitive souls

TARA JACKSON

Very best wishes,
Tara
x

Dedication

This book is dedicated to you, dad.

You picked me from the clinic in Delhi and I'm forever grateful you did. We have been through so much together, and I would not be the person I am today without your eternal support and love. I am so thankful for our whole journey – the good, the messy, the fun, the difficult, the incredible, the hard parts – all of it!

Thank you for being YOU: the silly, funny, unique and incredibly generous person that you are! Thank you for always encouraging me to follow my own path and thank you for always believing in me, even when I didn't. Especially when I didn't.

I am forever grateful to have you as my dad and I wouldn't be me without you!

Love you.

Praise for Embodied

With courage and honesty, Tara shares her journey and offers sincere and relatable advice to anyone who needs a hand in that most important of acts: self-care.
Alice McGurran, Editor, www.welldoing.org

Embodied had me both in tears and laughter within the first few pages! The combination of Tara's personal story with the 52 self-care tips is incredibly powerful. This book is a gateway to deeper levels of self-care for women at all stages of their life journey.
Nicola Humber, Author of 'Unbound' and 'Heal Your Inner Good Girl'

Embodied is an incredibly raw, real and much-needed offering from a wonderfully wise and kind soul. Paving the way for women, and men to share their stories without a filter, to describe their truth and embrace their shadow. A must read for those with the understanding that it is through telling our stories with authenticity and courage, that the world becomes a much smaller and kinder place.
Julia Tobin, Creator, www.glowfromtheinsideout.com

Contents

Introduction and how to use this book

Welcome,

It is so great to have you here, holding this book in your hands. It is the culmination of a long journey of trial and error, of looking and searching within, finding answers and healing. I am honoured to be able to share it with you.

I have written this book to share my self-care journey as a highly sensitive empath. It is for you if you are also sensitive to all that goes on around you and may be struggling with your own self-care. You might be battling with addictions and numbing yourself, you may be feeling like you are all alone in how you feel, your wellbeing might be suffering, or perhaps you are simply looking for some self-care inspiration as a sensitive person.

This book is split into two parts.

First is my story: the journey of my life so far, how I lost my way, went through years of self-abuse and addiction, anything to escape myself and my reality, living a life that I felt wasn't going anywhere.

I share it in the possibility that it will inspire you. Perhaps something in there will make you realise there is hope and that actually, turning things around may not be that far away from what you imagine.

In the second part there is a guide with 52 self-care actions/

inspirations/stories, one for every week of the year if you choose, that I have personally used (and still use today). They include a mix of external actions – ones I used more at the beginning of my journey as I needed something more outward 'to do', as well as things to help you look inside.

Some are foundational ones, like eating well and moving your body. The rest can be seen more like a pick 'n' mix of ones to perhaps randomly choose from and go back to. I find that I go through phases when some are more relevant to me and I will practice them daily until I embody them. You'll likely find things in there that you already know, but we can all do with reminders... I find that lessons will reappear again and again until you learn them, until they have passed through you.

There is a mix of tips, lessons, suggestions, intuitive guidance and words I received as I was healing, to hopefully inspire and motivate you. If something doesn't immediately resonate, leave it, perhaps come back to it again, but maybe it's also not for you. This journey is about finding out what works for you!

Self-care is an ongoing journey, there really is no end point, as it took me years to learn. I commit daily to myself and my self-care and my hope is that this book will inspire you to do the same.

If you have 'off' days or even weeks, that's okay. Please don't be hard on yourself, be gentle and compassionate – we are all doing our best and all on different paths. Just keep coming back, revisit your reasons for doing this all in the first place, and get support (whether it be from friends, family, a coach, therapist, even your dog to begin), we really don't have to do this journey on our own.

I wish you a life filled with more self-care, compassion and love, and ultimately, a life where you can be fully expressed in your beautiful body.

Much love to you,

Tara

PART ONE – MY STORY

Before I begin, I would like to say that this story is my perspective and version on my life and how things unfolded. I am so grateful for everything and everyone in my life and I wouldn't be here sharing this book if it weren't for all of it.

Coming into this world

It was a warm September morning and the sun was just beginning to rise in New Delhi, on the day I came into the world. My biological mother was a young 15-year-old who had travelled to New Delhi especially for the birth, as she couldn't keep me, and this was a place where finding another parent for her unborn child was possible.

I am still not sure of the exact reasons why she needed to give me up, but I know that my biological father was her maths tutor and there must have been some, if not a lot of, controversy surrounding the situation.

At the same time, my parents, originally from the UK and Canada, decided to do some travelling before each starting various contracts with the UN in Nairobi, Kenya. They had stopped off to see some friends in New Delhi, before going trekking in Nepal, and as they were unable to have children decided they wanted to adopt from somewhere along their travels. One of the friends was a social worker and knew a lawyer who handled adoptions, so she put them in touch. After meeting the lawyer, he then passed them on to a doctor at a nursing home in eastern New Delhi. They met her and chatted a bit, agreeing to be in touch

TARA JACKSON

after they returned in a couple of weeks' time.

After a magical trip trekking, they had returned to Delhi and were about to leave for the airport to go back to Nairobi, when they remembered that they had said they'd be in touch with the clinic. They called the nurse and she told them she had a baby girl for them, right then!

Not wanting to miss this opportunity, they took a tuk tuk to the baby care shop and bought six baby bottles and six nappies before heading to the clinic. When they got there another baby girl had been born. My dad was holding one and my mum the other. The doctor said they could take both. My parents looked at each other a bit overwhelmed and asked which one had been born first, when they had called, as they wanted to have more children but spaced out a bit, having not even known they'd have one that morning!

My dad happened to be holding the first born – which was me, and they said we'll take that one. They signed a paper giving them guardianship, along with a Catholic nun as the local guardian. Then off they went in another tuk tuk back to their friend's house.

Trying to feed me they realised the baby bottle nipples had no holes in and that you had to make your own. One of their friend's was a former nuclear physicist which seemed to be no help at all! They ruined the first five nipples making them too small or too big and had me either screaming with hunger or choking as the milk flooded out... The last chance was with the sixth and final nipple and they used the pin of a brooch heated on the

2

gas stove ring to get it right...whew, it worked! I got milk finally!

So, having managed to feed me, they decided to go to a hotel to celebrate. They asked for a bottle of champagne, but it was too expensive. They then asked for a bottle of wine – same thing, it was too much. So, they opted for a beer each as they wanted to celebrate that they were now parents. They did. They each had their beer and left the restaurant.

But as they left the restaurant excited and about to leave in their tuk tuk, they forgot one little thing asleep under the table... me! Most parents get nine months to prepare for a baby, they hadn't even had a full day. They rushed back to collect their newest addition.

They had to stay in Delhi a bit longer now as I needed a passport in my own name to be able to travel back with them. They'd decided on my name, it was Meera, and they were about to finalise all the paperwork, but, with their friends one evening on the rooftop cooling off from the hot day, they were all looking up at the stars. Mesmerised as most are by the stars in India, my parents asked their friends what star was in Hindi – 'Tara', they replied. That was beautiful they decided, so they changed my name to 'Tara'. The name 'Tara' also had connections to the High Kings of Ireland, so that was an extra plus for my mum, being half Irish.

The lawyer then advised them to backdate my birthday to make it seem like no Indian parents had come forward to adopt, so it would be okay for foreigners to do so, and I could leave the country with them. So, they did and back we all flew together, to the new house in Nairobi – a huge place on 25 acres of land, built by a wildlife filmmaker.

A year later my parents returned to India for another child, my sister, and a year after that another, my brother, each from different families but at the same clinic.

Even though we weren't all legally adopted until years later, my parents were our legal guardians along with the Catholic sister in New Delhi. After lots of letters, phone calls and faxes between the doctor, the lawyers and institutions in India, Kenya, the UK and Canada, they needed to be interviewed and have a home study done to ascertain that they were suitable parents. The woman who was interviewing came to the house and was afraid to get out of the car in case there were lions. But she was happy with what she saw and wrote a letter stating that Mr. and Mrs. Jackson were very nice people, that the house had 4 bedrooms, a swimming pool and 12 chickens so the children would not be wanting for eggs. That was it. We were legally adopted by my mum and dad.

The early years

I had an idyllic childhood. I had friends from down the road that I would bike ride with, friends that came to stay, birthday parties with lots of friends, food and presents. A magical garden on my doorstep with tonnes of different types of flowers, fruits, a pond, a mini forest, an outdoor playground with a climbing frame, swings and a little swimming pool down some windy stone steps from the house. I had loving parents who were in and out of the house as they both worked a lot, a younger sister

4

and brother to play with, and even my own nanny to look after me. There was everything you could possibly want as a child.

I loved kindergarten and was an outgoing, confident child who asked for what she wanted. I loved acting and being the centre of attention and remember being in a lot of plays as well as making up my own at home, forcing my younger siblings to take part. But I also loved spending hours on my own exploring or swimming. I remember fully believing in magic as a child and when I was in the garden I felt that there were fairies and other mythical beings with me. I'd tell myself stories as I wandered around. The swimming pool was also my own magical little world and I would pretend to be a mermaid swimming for hours at a time whenever I could.

I was extremely lucky and privileged to have all of those things and even though I didn't know any different, I took full advantage of my situation. There was so much to be thankful for. So much in that world that I didn't even realise wasn't the norm until much later in life. I guess you only know what you know, and that was my reality, a wonderful few years where my world really was a magical place.

Things started to change

When I was seven my mum got sick. I don't really remember the exact details, but what I do remember is my dad saying that it would be good if she didn't have to drive so much every day. We lived on the other side of Nairobi from where she worked and although where we lived was close to our school and kindergarten, she was having to drive over an hour each way in the mad, rush hour traffic and we'd not see much of her as she was gone for such long hours.

So, we moved houses to be nearer where she worked. It was going to help. It meant less travelling for her.

The new house was nice, the garden was a lot smaller and to my personal dismay there was no swimming pool, but there were raspberries growing in the garden, and that I liked! I also now lived closer to one of my best friends, so I decided it was going to be fun.

But it didn't last for long. Shortly after we'd moved my mum had to go to the UK for treatment, and not long after my dad said the rest of us were going to join her. We didn't really know what that meant, but we'd be living near our grandmother, on the outskirts of London, and we had some friends from Kenya and family there, so it sounded like it would be alright.

Life in the UK began.

My sister and I went to the same all girls Convent school which my mum and her sister had gone to as children. My younger brother was in an all-boys school. It didn't feel that different from school in Kenya. School was busy and we spent weekends with my granny who lived nearby, or friends, it was very full on but also fun.

My dad was around a lot more than he had been in Kenya, he was the one mainly looking after us. He'd drive us to school and friend's houses and cook and clean. It was cool having him around more. He would let us get away with more than our mum. I remember wanting to get my hair cut and she had said no, so I asked my dad and he let me get it all cut off in a tiny little bob, much to her disapproval. I loved it!

Life went by and everything seemed to be good. But meanwhile my mum was getting sicker and spending more and more time in the hospital in London.

Then one day, and I remember it vividly, we had just left the hospital after visiting my mum and were on our way to see some old family friends who had been in Kenya, but now lived in the UK. Our dad turned to us in the car and said your mum isn't going to make it. She is really sick and isn't going to live. My brother and sister, in the back seat, started crying – but I didn't. I remember thinking WHAT? No. I don't believe it, it's not real. This isn't the way it has to be. It felt so surreal.

I brushed it aside not really understanding what it meant. How can you imagine what life will be like without a parent as an eight-year-old? I don't think you can really. We got to our friend's house and carried on like it wasn't real. It almost felt like I had imagined the whole conversation. Did it actually happen?

From then onwards we had lots of our family from all over the world come to stay at different times. Aunts, uncles, cousins, grandparents – my mum's family who lived in the UK, my dad's family from the US and Rome – all of them around to play with and look after us. It was fun having everyone there, it distracted from what was really going on.

One of my cousin's and I decided to build a dolls house out of shoe boxes, paper and whatever bits we could find lying around. It started as three shoe boxes layered on top of each other to make a three-story house. We made furniture, a TV, and beds out of coloured paper, scrap bits of materials and the inside of toilet rolls. Then we got more adventurous, I think we added a roof terrace, there was a winding staircase going up the side, we stuck it all on to a big board, so that it could have a garden with trees and a swimming pool (a blue piece of paper cut out). The last thing we added, well my cousin being a guy in his teens did, was a little skateboard! The whole house was quite an achievement and we were both proud of it.

There were some great times with family and having lived all my life previously with just my dad, mum, brother and sister, it was nice having all of our relatives around.

Having a snowy Christmas was a magical experience, and in the few days after Christmas before New Year we went to Paris.

We drove there from our home – it was us three kids, my mum, dad and our aunt too, taking the ferry from Dover. I remember it being rocky on the ferry and when we got there, there were a few complications with parking and the hotel, but they were all sorted and when we all went out together, we ate seafood, we walked around cobbled streets and it rained quite a bit. There was also the feeling of it being a significant trip, that in hindsight, I realised would be our last.

After that, things are kind of a blur, it was January, cold and grey. We were still in school and my mum was having to stay in the hospital more. My dad's mum, our grandma, was over to be with us at home, as my dad was with my mum.

I remember the day we went to the hospital to say goodbye. She was lying there, in a coma, but she could have been sleeping. It looked like mum and it was her, but it didn't feel like her... I remember not really knowing what to feel, it didn't seem real.

We kissed her and said goodbye.

When my granny and aunt, her mum and sister, said goodbye she woke for a few minutes to say goodbye to them.

Not long after that, a couple of days after Valentine's Day (we knew as my grandma had been building a special Valentine's Day snow-woman with us in the back garden!), my dad came home from the hospital and told us that our mum had died. Seeing her in the hospital those days before wasn't real. This seemed even less real.

It was quite a whirlwind from then onwards. Next was my mum's funeral, which more family came over for. I read a passage at the service, which I practiced with my grandma and uncle.

When we watched her being buried it became more real. Watching everyone's grief was overwhelming. I remember holding on to my aunt, crying into her, so I didn't have to see what was going on.

My mum was gone.

Back in Kenya

After my mum passed away, it was one of those turning points where everything changes overnight and life as you know it won't ever be the same again. It can't be. At the time I didn't really know what had happened. I knew my mum had gone and that things would be a bit different, but I didn't expect it to unravel in the way that it did.

We moved back to Kenya, via Rome, to stay with my dad's sister – my aunt, uncle and cousin. Rome was great, it felt like a holiday still. We were in transition, still in the aftermath of what had actually happened. In hindsight it probably hadn't really, really hit any of us yet.

But when we got back to our home in Kenya, the reality started to sink in. The hardest part, you realise later, is the bit when everyone has gone. When there are no more distractions and you are left to get on with life as 'normal'.

I remember thinking that it would be similar, just minus mum. That dad would still be dad, we'd go back to school and get on with life. We were in the same house, so that was a constant. We had an amazing lady who helped at home and had been with us since before we went to the UK. Mum had been working so much and hadn't been there as much recently, so in my heart I thought things wouldn't be all that different. But they were.

There were mixed feelings being back. I was happy being back in Kenya, in the country that was my home and with friends that I had missed. Our school was amazing, they had made my brother, sister and I all personalised blankets to show their support and I remember feeling loved. But at the same time, I didn't want to be pitied for not having a mum now. Not at all.

I remember my mum's death being one of those things that you don't really talk about, it had just happened and that's the way it was. I don't remember ever crying (at least not to anyone else) and it wasn't something that you could easily bring up. I was so young at the time; I think people sort of just assumed I would be okay and get on with everything. When people asked about my family, I'd just brush off the fact that my mother had passed away as though it didn't bother me in the slightest. It was just a fact, and that was it. I was fine and felt like if life returned to the way it was, all would be good. A little part inside me didn't really want to believe she was fully gone either. In my head, I imagined she'd come back walking through the door one day, or we'd see her out and about.

As the days and weeks went on, my dad began drinking in the evenings. A lot. He drank and played music all the time. Lots of Queen. He'd fall asleep with Queen playing, blasting from the speakers even, and I'd come down, from trying to sleep, late into the night and would have to turn off the music, lock up the house and help him up to bed, if I could.

I didn't really know what was going on. It felt upsetting and confusing to me; all I knew was this wasn't the dad I knew. The calm and put together dad, who had been there so much for us in the UK. He was crumbling and I wasn't sure what to do. My little brother and sister were there, my sister got on as she always did, but my brother was more vocal about hating the change. I remember feeling I had to protect them, I didn't want them to see our dad like that. Night after night, doing what he needed to, to deal with his pain.

A different side to him came out, a side I'd never seen before. He began to drown his pain in the only way he knew how. It was difficult seeing that and I got so angry at him for acting so out of control. For not being the dad he had always been. For changing so abruptly and for seemingly not realising that it was affecting us. His music is the thing I remember the most. It was loud and desperate. Desperate for a life that was no longer. I also began to resent him as he seemed unable to control himself and it became so unpredictable at home. I began to hate being there. I didn't know when he'd be drinking and when he wouldn't. He became the opposite of the person I knew and loved, the dad who used to let me into his darkroom when he was working and show me his photos, the dad that had an awesome fish tank, which I could stare at for hours.

When he started to date, I remember feeling so confused and angry. My brother, sister and I hadn't got over the death of our mother, why had he?! One of the first times I saw him with someone else in his bed (I walked in unannounced one morning) I ran screaming to some family friends who lived nearby. It felt wrong seeing him with someone else. I lead the others in making the women he saw lives' hell! We would put their toothbrushes in the toilet, hide their things or even put lipstick on their clothes. I wasn't ready for any of that. I didn't want or need a new mum and I wasn't going to play nice!

There was some respite at times, and I know he was trying.

He still loved us and was our dad. There would be moments when we would do fun things together and he'd get us up for school, eat breakfast with us – making sure we each had half a grapefruit and a piece of toast, and he would be there to pick us up from the bus stop after school where we would do the grocery shopping together. We'd always be allowed to pick the fruits we liked, like passion fruits, mangoes, custard apple or guavas, depending on what was in season.

I remember him letting me miss school one day as I was feeling tired and just needed a break from it all. He wrote a letter to my teacher being honest about the reason. I got into trouble for it, which I didn't understand at all. I thought it was a cool thing for him to do and was thankful for it.

But there was a lot of unpredictability at home too. We'd go through periods with tonnes of people in and out of our house. Lodgers, friends, randoms. It became this party zone that was loud and messy, and I just found it all too much. In some ways I found relief when we had others to stay, it meant I didn't have to take care of dad, put him to bed if needed, or make sure the house was locked up. But it was always so busy – you never knew what to expect. There was also always lots of drinking and I didn't like being around it. I didn't like what it did to people, what they became, especially my dad.

I remember one weekend when we had been with some friends who lived near a coffee plantation in the middle of nowhere. There had been a lot of drinking amongst the adults and we'd been playing with the other kids. We were going to stay the night, one of the other parents thought it would be best, but my dad insisted on driving home. It was a long scary journey back. The roads were long and dark, many had potholes and there weren't streetlights for the most part. I was sitting in the front seat, my brother and sister in the back, half asleep. My dad was in and out, swerving so much I ended up having to help steer, not sure if we would make it home.

I found it exhausting. I was angry at my dad. Angry he was acting so useless. I just wanted a 'normal', peaceful life, whatever that was. I felt like nobody understood, I had so much frustration and confusion building inside with no place for it to go.

I wanted to be at my friends' houses whenever I could – weekends, even school nights if I could come up with a good enough reason (staying after team matches was one I used the most). Their homes all felt so much more stable than mine. I would have friends over sometimes; we'd make up plays and pretend to be Teenage Mutant Ninja Turtles. But I was always on edge. Scared my dad would start drinking and saying things that I found embarrassing.

I also felt different from my sister and brother who over time, seemed to me, to mesh so much more easily into the chaotic life that had become our home. They seemed happy to have lots of people around all the time and go to bed at weird hours. I felt so unsettled and overwhelmed, and all I wanted was quiet and consistency.

When I did have to be at home alone I would escape in my books. Books about magic, childhoods which were crappy then turned out okay – anything by Roald Dahl (and particularly Matilda), stories where there were things out of this realm, possibilities, magic, hope... Books were my sanctuary and I would be in my room reading all the time, apart from at meal times.

I also found relief in the summer holidays when we would spend them with our extended family in the US, Canada and Europe: my grandparents, aunts, uncles and cousins. I could be a kid again and I particularly loved staying with my grandma and grandpa (my dad's mum and dad) as my dad calmed around them and it felt a bit like having a mum again for us too.

Our awesome cousins also spoiled us and we had so much fun hanging out and getting to do things which weren't really around in Kenya at the time, like seeing movies, shopping in trendy London shops or visiting cool US malls, having big, fun family meals together, swimming in the lake and going out for ice cream.

When we stayed at my grandparents' I remember all the things I loved doing would happen – it was like being a child in a magical kingdom again. Our grandpa would take us to the library, and I'd get out the maximum 50 books for the few weeks we'd be there – and they would easily all be finished before we left. We would help our grandma in her garden; she had lots of fruits and vegetables growing – pears, apples, strawberries, arugula (rocket), but her cherry tomatoes were her pride and joy. She'd grow them from seed each year and they were the ripest, sweetest, little red balls of deliciousness. She'd let us water them with her and of course eat a few. We'd get to watch American TV shows – with our favourite (also one my grandma approved of) being Saved by the Bell. I'd also play games with my sister and brother, something we didn't do as much of together in Kenya. I would make them play 'offices' with me, where we'd pretend we were all working in different rooms and put little pieces of paper under each other's doors for 'meetings'. I'm not sure what we actually did, but it felt fun and very important at the time (maybe more to me than my brother and sister).

It was always sad leaving them all after the summers and whilst I got by in Kenya and loved my school life and friends, deep down inside I felt different from everyone. My home life seemed like such a mess compared to everyone else's. I was also in pain, although I swallowed back any feelings of sadness that ever started to rise. Everything had to stay inside or be pushed back down if it ever seemed like it might surface, so I wouldn't have to feel it. The only thing that was allowed to come out was anger, and it did at my dad, a lot. I remember feeling like I was two different people – one at home and one at school.

I didn't allow myself, or even really know how, to process the changes, so life just went on and this was how I adapted.

Family changing

When I was 11, my dad met someone who would later become my stepmother. She had been visiting Kenya with work and pretty much moved in with us within a couple of weeks as she didn't have her own place. She was much nicer than the other girlfriends my dad had had, and it felt safe having her around.

After this her two young children came over to Kenya to join and then with my dad, she fell pregnant with twins. We went from three children to seven almost overnight. Especially as the twins were three months premature.

It all happened so quickly I don't think any of us knew how to feel. On the one hand it was great having another adult around and for the most part (or at least in the beginning) my dad seemed to drink less. But it also unsettled things as I had to give up my bedroom and move into the garage with my sister, which was converted into a little house for us.

At first, I hated it, it smelled different and was really close to the elements – we'd get gecko poop all over our things and weird little creatures in our room. But after a while I grew to love it – it was an escape from the main house and all that went on in there. I found it a little sanctuary and it was so nice to have somewhere peaceful that was just ours. We had big windows that looked out over the garden and onto the forest at the bottom, with monkeys that would regularly come by around sunset and jump on the roof. We'd even get peeping monkeys and have to remember to shut our curtains as there was one in particular that used to stare in and I caught him watching me one time when I was changing (no joke)! We had an old TV and video player, so we'd watch countless episodes of Friends late into the night when we weren't allowed and would hide snacks in our drawers for late night feasts. In my teens I'd sneak out with friends, getting my sister to cover for me. We also had quite a few small 'parties' without anyone knowing. It really was a great place to live in.

I also loved having all the little ones around. In a way they became a security blanket for me. I found it so much easier to be around them than the adults. I'd always opt to look after them and I'd often be left at home with them when the others went out, or even when we had guests over. With the younger children I felt relaxed and like I could just be me. We'd also play games and watch cartoons together, which was a nice escape. My step mum's two would spend the holidays with their dad in Germany and they would always bring us back lots of German chocolates and sweets like Milka bars and gummy bears, which I loved.

I also enjoyed the praise I got from being the one to help look after the younger siblings. In a house with so many children it was often hard to get attention and as the good, elder sister who could be relied upon to be there, this was certainly a way.

Even though there was more stability, it still felt weird at home. Things were different and no matter how hard I tried to act like everything was normal and how this new family was great, inside I still felt so confused. It felt like my brother, sister and I were just there – with this whole other family. A part of me wanted it to just be dad and the three of us, whilst another part enjoyed having this big mixed up family. It was definitely a big adjustment and another thing I just got on with as best as I could.

Finding comfort in food

Looking back, I realise I left my body when my mum died. I escaped into my head, my mind, a place where I could choose to be what I wanted and choose to remember what I wanted, I could escape. In here it was easier to ignore the feelings my body felt. I didn't trust my body any longer, I didn't want to be connected with it.

I also began to find that food helped with this and made me feel better. It gave me a sense of security, comfort and happiness for the moments it lasted. I found that eating cakes gave me a warm, fuzzy inner feeling – something I rarely felt. They also filled me right up, not leaving any space for me to feel anything else. It was the perfect combination of feeling full and heavy, and not able to connect with any emotion going on.

I remember the rush I got when I had something sugary, I'd feel full, satisfied and buzzing. It would make the anger dissipate and I wouldn't feel so pissed off with everything going on. This would last for a few hours but then I'd inevitably crash and want more.

With the eating I also found I could numb any kind of feeling I was having, especially anything I felt was negative; anything sad, lonely, angry, confused, anything that wasn't 'normal' and happy, which I didn't want to feel. So, I began to use this 'tool' for everything, all of my feelings that I didn't want to come up.

I remember there was a time, a few days, where I felt like crying so desperately because I felt so fed up, misunderstood, alone and sad, but I couldn't show it. I couldn't let anyone see. Nor did I feel like I had anyone to be there if I did. So, at the next opportunity I got, on the way home from school, I snuck into a candy shop with pick 'n' mix sweets and bought as many as I could buy with 500 shillings (a lot at the time), which was about £5. I got a stripy paper bag filled with a good few handfuls of chocolate, toffees, fudges and other creamy sweets. When I got home, I shut myself away in my room with the bag of candy. I took the cellophane and silver wrappers off each piece as fast as I could, then laid them out in front of me. Then I shovelled each piece into my mouth, one by one, but not stopping to finish before the next one went in so my whole mouth was almost full, barely chewing, it was like I was on autopilot, stuffing down the pain. I didn't feel anything; I tasted the sugariness, but I was just using it to absorb the building tears and numb any feelings that were rising. They were too painful, and I didn't want to experience them.

It worked. The candy lifted me, took me away from my body, and the feelings that were rising disappeared, buried even deeper.

My love for cooking

My love for cooking and being in the kitchen started alongside my love for eating. We weren't actually allowed much junk food or sweet things at home, even though I managed to sneak them in. I got around this by saying I wanted to cook (thereby doing something creative that my parents approved of), and then I would try to bake something, which would satisfy my young sweet tooth.

My first creations were awful! I remember a friend coming over and we made a chocolate cake, which looked more like the terrain on Mars with its valleys and mountains, dips and crevasses, and tasted like an old, hard, flavourless sponge.

I kept on trying. My craving for sugary baked treats wasn't going to let my amateur cooking skills get in the way. With the help of a wonderful cooking book from my godmother, with lots of inspiring pictures, I did progress. I found that making chocolate cornflakes was a lot easier (and harder to get wrong), and it produced a tasty, chocolatey, gooey snack that hit the sweet spot and numbed any feelings I was trying to escape.

Even then, I remember finding a therapeutic almost methodical peace in the process of cooking. So, I kept going with my baking experiments and by the time I reached my teens I was making meringues, cakes, cheesecakes and a number of other delicious desserts.

I then started to spend a lot more time at my best friend's house and this is where I started to learn how to cook savoury dishes and fell in love with all kinds of ingredients and flavours. My friend's mum cooked every meal from scratch, and being from India this included lots of vegetables, spices, breads, fresh herbs, and more. Their store cupboard was full of the most amazing treasures you could imagine – pickles, colourful looking spices with strange smells, snacks I had never seen before, grains piled up high, and jars and tins with things in I couldn't identify. It was amazing.

I'd watch my friend's mum sauté garlic, onions, ginger, chillies and add different spices then the vegetables, each time producing something different but delicious. I was truly in food heaven. This love for cooking stuck with me from then. In a way it gave me a creative release, and I came back to it later in life.

Teen years

As we all got older, home life became a regimented kind of affair. As there were seven children, all with different schedules (at one point we were in five different schools), it was a lot to keep on top of. It felt more like a system than a home life and whilst my parents each did their best in their own ways, I remember wanting to spend as little time with them as possible. Perhaps not so unusual for a teen to be honest!

I still loved school and my friends, I loved all the sports I did, the teams I played for, and I loved learning. Anything to escape into another world and fill myself up in some way as I was used to doing by now. Art was a safe space for me too. I could spend hours drawing all of the beautiful flowers and plants at school and at home. Being in that world was sheer relaxation for me and hours would easily pass by.

The rest of my life began to revolve around food and where and what I was going to eat next. All of my pocket money went on junk food – chicken pies and brownies from the bakery after school, bags of crisps, Kit Kats, Twixs and sodas from the tuck shop, French fries, fried chicken, subs, ice cream and pizza from the new mall that had opened and where I spent time with friends on weekends. I wouldn't savour whatever I bought either, I would eat it as fast as I could. One break time I remember even 'showing off' about how fast I could shovel down a bag of skittles and then gulp down a bottle of cola, then I'd get super hyper and silly, which I enjoyed, until it wore off and I crashed. I never got full either. On weekends I could easily have two lunches when I went out with my friends – fried chicken and chips, then a pizza, then ice cream and even want more.

At home dinner was mostly vegetarian, which I hated! It didn't give me the same sense of fullness I got from meat and carbs. I would complain about it, push around a few pieces of broccoli and then secretly order pizza and subs from the one takeaway place there was, once we were allowed to leave the table, and if I had any money. On weekends we would sometimes go to the UN commissary with my dad, that would be another opportunity for more candy. We were usually allowed one thing each, but rather than pick one small candy bar, it would be a multi pack, which 'technically' was still one bag, so that counted! Whatever I chose that weekend would be gone by Monday, it was unlikely it would even last that long.

Life became about food and finding ways to get sweet, fatty or salty foods inside of me. They made me feel warm and fuzzy, happy even; I felt good about myself while it lasted.

But, at this time I was also becoming increasingly more aware of my body. I was in a bit of an awkward phase, quite tall, not yet fully holding myself. Hips and bum getting bigger, boobs starting to grow, hair starting to sprout in places I didn't want it to. It was weird having all these changes happening and not really knowing how to feel about them. I was also one of the bigger girls in my year and felt like I stood out. Friends, who I thought were the slim, pretty girls, were starting to date and I just didn't think I ever would if I didn't look like them. More fuel to aid my thinking was that my younger sister by a year, who had also started dating a bit, had a tiny petite build; that made my young and vulnerable self, feel even fatter.

I felt like I would never be happy at my size. So began my quest for ways to make myself smaller and mould into what I believed was the 'right' size and shape.

The first was starving myself. Breakfast was easy to skip as by this time I was the only one going to secondary school in the family and I was getting up earlier than everyone else to make it on time. School lunches were a chilled affair so we could choose whether we wanted to eat or not. In the evenings at home, or at meals on weekends, I'd pretend to eat, but secretly hide my food in napkins and then flush it down the toilet. It was also really easy to throw food into the garden in the plants where nobody would see it. I'd say I had a huge lunch at school, so I didn't have to eat dinner. It also helped having so many children as the attention wouldn't be on any of us for too long, or it would be mainly on the twins who were toddlers and still needed feeding.

When I first began monitoring what I did and didn't eat, it felt good. I got such a rush off the secrecy. I also felt myself getting slimmer and I felt so in control – something I wasn't used to feeling, it was nice. But with that I lost out on some of the hyper feelings I felt off sugar and I began to crave it. With the little food I was consuming, teen hormones pumping, feelings of emptiness and cravings for food and sugar, I was all over the place! I don't know how I held it together. Then one day in the school bathrooms I heard about someone who had made herself sick after eating, so she could still eat what she wanted and lose weight. A lightbulb went off in my head. I missed food! I loved the taste and texture, I loved feeling full up.

I got to go back to stuffing myself with all the things I loved, all the sugar, all the pizza, even meals at home, then I would excuse myself from the table, go to a bathroom where I knew nobody could hear, put two of my fingers down my throat as far back as I could reach, ignoring any gagging, I'd feel my stomach contract and force what I'd eaten back up. I got to feel full, numb and satiated, then I got to feel empty and in control again. I felt like I had found the answer.

It was such a sad, vicious cycle that began to consume me. Even though I thought I was totally in control, I wasn't. The smallest thing I ate I knew was going to come back up. I became obsessive, needing to know where the bathrooms were if I was ever going to eat. I couldn't go to friend's houses as much either as I didn't want anyone to know what I was doing.

At the same time, I began exercising like crazy. I'd do hundreds of sit ups, leg raises and other toning exercises religiously before bed every night, plus I'd get up extra early to repeat the same sequences. At school I was doing at least an hour of sport a day too. But it was never enough, I couldn't re-shape and control my body as fast or as much as I wanted to.

This made me feel powerless and begin to hate myself as I wasn't 'where' I wanted to be. I would look at myself in the mirror at every opportunity, to see if there was more fat sticking out, or if I looked different from when I'd checked an hour ago. Sometimes I'd weight myself a few times a day, hoping for a difference. I'd pull back any 'softer' parts, like on my thighs or my cheekbones, imagining how I'd look if they were gone.

I remember wanting people to comment on how thin I was

getting, especially my parents, but they didn't really notice. Looking back now, all I wanted was care and attention. My best friend was worried though as she knew what was happening and I am so grateful to her for caring about me as it felt like some acknowledgment.

Although the eating disorder didn't stop for a while, it didn't have a distinct end point, I just remember it became less of a focus as I moved into the final two years of secondary school. I had also started getting dizzy spells so was finding I actually needed to eat, or I couldn't play sport, which I loved. Plus, constantly having to hide everything and be near a bathroom was getting exhausting. But I would still go through mini phases of eating too much, then purging, or phases of restricting myself, which continued even for the next decade or so of my life.

Back to the UK for university

After secondary school, the 'done' thing was to go abroad for university. I wasn't ready for that yet; I didn't want to leave all that I knew in Kenya. I also didn't know what I wanted to study or do 'when I grew up'. I had done art for one of my A-levels in school and having 'missed' (on purpose) the deadline for UCAS (the system to apply for 'regular' degrees at UK universities), I was left with the second option of applying for art schools. I had offers from a few but had decided on London as this was where two of my close friends also decided to go, and it would be a lot less cold than Glasgow, which was the other offer I was considering.

When I got to London I was shocked by how busy and crowded it was, more than anything. The madness of it all intimidated me. I'd visited family and family friends in the UK over the years, but that had been in a safe, protected bubble with people that knew London and would be there to show me around. This time, I was on my own, to fend for myself and I felt like a small-town child in a big, scary city.

I had the assumed safety blanket of my university, but it too was different from anything I had imagined. There was no campus life and everything within easy walking distance, with shops, a library etc right on hand, like you see in the movies. No, this was London, and I had to find my way around as Londoners did. At the time it felt like a cold harsh reality check that I needed to grow up.

The first time I got on a bus, I got in the back entrance and the driver yelled at me, I felt humiliated and scared. It also overwhelmed me, and I was quite nervous about doing anything for a long time after that, and I didn't think I'd ever fit in! But, as with all things, I started to figure it out and find my way around. I felt quite proud of myself as I learned where to do laundry (in the Laundromat down the road), buy groceries (where the supermarkets and corner shops were near my university and halls of residence were) and which buses to take to get to my different classes.

But, alongside this little victory for me, my homesickness was beginning to consume me. On days I had classes I would be distracted and immerse myself in what I was doing – although, not very well as I was feeling so low inside. But still it was a distraction. On other days I would watch TV all day long –

countless episodes of Sabrina the teenage witch on repeat.

It was getting colder and colder outside, and the dark nights were getting longer. I found the fact that the sun had no warmth really strange and I didn't like that the leaves were all falling from the trees. Being a tropical girl inside, this was not something my body was used to. I was cold and could feel what I later learned was seasonal affective disorder creeping up on me. I felt low and all I wanted to do was eat and sleep.

That's what I did. I began to eat and drink excessively. If it was a quick and easy white carbohydrate, I was on it. On days after class when I had found the energy to hang out with a friend, we'd go to Starbucks and have a creamy coffee with sugar, a toasted panini with ham and mozzarella followed by a muffin. Or if I wanted to get back into the safety and warmth of my bed in front of my TV (which was often), I'd stop by the bigger corner shop and buy a warm baguette with a couple of cans of pre-mixed tuna, sweetcorn and mayo, with a couple of chocolate bars for after. I'd get back to my halls of residence, quickly (whilst the bread was still warm) mix the tuna up and slather it inside the baguette. Cut the baguette in half, saying I'd save one for later (I never did), and curl up in my duvet watching a comforting teenage show while I guzzled the baguette and chocolates, mindlessly, barely touching the sides.

During this time, I also wasn't exercising. I used to do almost daily sport at school in Kenya but there was no way I was going outside in the cold to exercise and I was too shy to join a gym.

I grew more and more disconnected from my body as I ate

more, moved less, and started wearing all black, baggy clothes to drown me out, reflect my mood, and blend in with the surroundings (or how they appeared to me). I gained about 10kgs in my first year of university – a layer that protected and comforted me during that time.

I sometimes feel I made it harder for myself than it needed to be. I resisted being there so much. I didn't want to like it and I'd literally cross off the days on my little wall calendar, counting down the days until I would next be able to go home.

Feeling lost and unsure of my identity

Coupled with the homesickness I was becoming more aware of my identity, or 'confused identity' as I even named one of my first email addresses. I was repeatedly being asked to define my race when I filled in forms – like registering for the doctor and applying for a student card. It felt so weird to tick the box for 'Asian – Indian', when I didn't identify with this on the inside. I received my first racial abuse as a brown person, two teenage boys walked past me once, pushing me over and calling me 'Fucking Paki' as they did. I felt scared and angry – they didn't know who I was. I began to resent being brown as I began to associate that experience with the colour of my skin. I identified with so many things, so I started ticking the 'Other' box, thinking it would separate me from it and I hated having to answer questions about my identity.

I felt so disconnected for most of my university years. I made a few friends also from abroad, who also felt as homesick and rootless as I did. We bonded over our love of the tropics and dislike of London. I'd make the occasional effort to go out and see something new and I did see a lot of amazing art during that time. But I usually found I ended up back at home as it was quiet, safe and warm – I felt like I didn't belong and was never going to be a 'Londoner'. Instead I escaped in food, bottles of cheap red wine and cider, and smoking weed.

The weed began like most students in art college, a few harmless joints that actually opened the creative passages, lots of talking, laughing and then the munchies. Oh, the munchies! I'd easily consume an oven pizza, a few bags of crisps, bars of chocolates and at least half a tub of Haagen Daz ice cream. I had some fun nights with friends smoking weed but eventually it too became another way to escape and I began smoking it in the mornings before class, then missing the class or going there in a haze, not really knowing what was going on but feeling totally paranoid the entire time.

This led to another cycle of disliking myself for doing everything to excess. I couldn't seem to do things just once in a while. Every day I'd either want to drink or smoke or binge eat, or if I could it would be all three together. I'd gain weight and feel crap because I wasn't looking after myself, stop for a bit with tremendous will power, then do it all over again, as I began to feel things I didn't want to feel. And I would do anything to not feel what was bubbling away under the surface, anything to not feel 'me'.

There'd be times when the hatred for my body shape and self would get too much and I'd buy a celebrity gossip magazine quickly turning to the pages with stories of how the latest 'C' list celeb had dropped three stone and how I could do it too. I'd jump on the bandwagon to try and lose some weight; thinking I'd have the perfect life if I just did this, and that I would feel amazing and happy in my body. I would follow it to the mark, lose a teensy bit of weight, then get frustrated it wasn't more and go back to my eating and gain it all back, plus more. Or a couple of times when I stuck with it a bit longer and did lose weight, I'd then think I could eat whatever I wanted as I was now thin. But of course, the weight always crept back on.

I look back and I wonder how I got through those years. There were definitely moments when I didn't want to be here. I saw no point, no purpose and thought there was nothing I had to give anyone, let alone myself. Nobody knew how sad I was inside, I'm sure it probably showed but I didn't talk to anyone about it. Even though I frequently thought about ending my life, I just knew I couldn't for my younger siblings. I knew I had to get through this, although I saw no light at the end of the tunnel. I didn't even remember what it felt like to wake up not feeling the emptiness and despondency that was my existence. I couldn't remember what genuine happiness felt like. Oh, how I missed my school days and life back in Kenya.

But things began to turn around after university when I started a full-time job. I started to have a reason to get up every morning, I had people who began to rely on me to come in and do my job. This gave me a purpose, a sense of belonging, I had some awesome work colleagues who became friends and I began to really enjoy the London social scene for the first time.

At this time I began living in a flat share close to central London.

Over the six years I lived there, I had flat mates from all over the world, and at one point I even lived with three of my close friends from school in Kenya. I definitely had some fun times but so many of them revolved around drinking, either at one of my favourite places on the nearby trendy high street with lots of bars and restaurants, or in our flat – where we could get bottles of red wine into the early hours from one of the many corner shops within a stone's throw of our front door.

However, I was still so confused inside, and work and my busy social life were just a distraction. I had no idea if this career path was for me, or if I even wanted a career path at all! I also didn't feel like I knew where home was. Yes, London was where I lived and I was actually getting out and having fun, but it didn't feel like home. I still found the city really overwhelming and I craved nature and the open spaces I had grown up with. I also had a lot of resentment and anger brewing from my childhood and wanted a break from all my family, so was less and less in touch, but that just isolated and confused me even further.

My solution was even more drinking. After work I would always manage to find someone who would be up for drinks with me. I loved that first sip of wine, which usually lead to a couple of bottles. It loosened me, I felt myself relaxing into my own being, settling into my body, I felt confident and like I fit in. I could share more openly and honestly; I could connect with others and not feel like I was holding back. I had some wonderful, deep conversations over wine, and I am very grateful for them. Looking back, they showed me that I was craving deep and meaningful connection, a way to be me, with people who got me, who experienced life like I did. I needed a release too and not knowing another way (or not wanting to find another way) that was what I sought.

It's such a shame I didn't know how to feel like I belonged or comfortable in my own skin without it, and I felt trapped and powerless to change it. Again, I fell into another vicious cycle where I would try and stop drinking for a few weeks, try and eat healthy or find a new diet to follow, resume exercising – by this time I had forced myself to join a gym – and I would notice some changes. I would start to feel a bit better, perhaps shed a bit of weight and there would be a glimmer of hope in the distance. Maybe I could like myself a bit, maybe things could change... But then as soon as this feeling came I would self-sabotage and go right back to drinking, and the hope and possibility I felt initially would fade.

I was an all or nothing person.

But, living this way year after year began to catch up with me. I could already feel how tired I was all the time and had started developing some digestive issues. They started small as most disease does – a few bouts of diarrhoea or vomiting and occasional pains. I ignored the symptoms, or masked them with anti-diarrhoea tablets, painkillers and other over the counter medications.

Eventually they got so bad I couldn't control when they would sneak up on me and once when out walking, I had to take a toilet break suddenly and URGENTLY, with nowhere to go but in my clothes. I was mortified and humiliated. How could this have happened to me? How did I let myself diarrhoea in my clothes and now I had to get home like this? Fortunately, I did, and I showered off embarrassed and in disbelief at what had just happened. After this I began to take taxis instead of public transport, in case I might need the bathroom suddenly, wasting a lot of money in the process. Sharing a flat was a nightmare as I'd feel panicky if anyone ever went into the one bathroom we all shared, in case I needed it.

I didn't know how I had let it get to this point. In hindsight, I did really, but I was in denial that my lifestyle had anything to do with it. I then started to see several doctors, going for blood tests, check-ups, allergy tests, anything to see whether there might be something wrong with my digestive system. The results all came back negative.

More self-destruction

I got to a point where I knew I didn't want to be doing what I had been. I couldn't go on any longer self-destructing and escaping. Things had reached a breaking point, I was finding it increasingly hard to hold it together, and I was physically crumbling. My digestive issues had reached their peak and I wouldn't leave the house unless I had taken anti-diarrhoea medication and knew where every bathroom would be. I knew where toilets were in tube stations, or hotels near tube stations that I could get to easily, if I ever went on the Underground. Even then I felt my anxiety rising and I was so on edge when I was travelling anywhere that I would try to not eat or drink anything for at least 2-3 hours beforehand.

I had been drinking copious amounts to try and feel something, to connect with a part of me that felt alive and felt love. This was followed with days of eating sometimes two breakfasts, lunch and then two dinners! I had no 'off' button and food was the quickest thing I could find that could both fill me up while simultaneously help me ignore anything I was feeling. Above all else, I really hated myself. I thought I was useless, a waste of space and a fat lump of a human being. I often wondered what the point of it all was, was this it, would I ever amount to anything, or was this going to be my life for however long I decided I wanted to be here.

Somewhere deep inside I knew there had to be more. In the 'up' moments when I'd looked after myself, I felt that there must be more for me. That somewhere out there was something I could be passionate about again. I had to make a change. I left my job not really knowing what I wanted to do, and I was unemployed for six months. Those six months started off okay. At first, I was determined to find something I liked, something that perhaps was similar to my last job but in the health and wellness field as I had always been interested in that. Even though I was always looking for new ways to lose weight I loved reading about how the body worked and how different foods fuelled it.

I applied to hundreds of jobs in that period but heard nothing back from any of them. I tried so hard to keep positive, to trust that something would come along. But it got harder as I began to max out all my credit cards and overdraft. Survival became the objective and I had to take the first job I was offered. I knew I didn't want it. It was highly administrative, and I felt myself die inside a little bit, wondering again if this was all there was and if I was crazy to think that it might not be.

At this time, I had moved in with an old friend, but it was a bit of a party flat, with lots of drugs and evenings spent drinking. I knew I couldn't go down that path, so at first, I resisted, but eventually my situation got the better of me and I needed an escape, so I tried my first bit of MDMA. It tasted disgusting, bitter and chemically, but when it kicked in, I felt that first rush lift me. I felt something inside that was familiar, that I hadn't felt in years, it was warm... fuzzy... comforting. It even felt like my heart was opening, I felt so much love and so connected to all of the people in the room. For a moment I forgot how much I hated myself and my situation. It was a wonderful feeling and I felt a glimmer that all was going to be okay.

The next day, however, I didn't feel so good. I felt my head screaming at me with self-loathing and negative thoughts. It was like the days when I was hungover and I'd hate myself, but this was worse! I felt paranoid, insecure and like I'd been 'too much'. I was so angry I'd let myself do drugs, I hated that I'd let myself share and be open with others in case I had embarrassed myself and been speaking a lot of rubbish. So, in the only way I knew how, I swore off everything and put myself on a harsh diet, cut myself off from everyone, watched TV to escape the thoughts and feelings, and tried to get back to normal. It took a few days, but eventually I did. As with the times I took off drinking I'd go through a phase of self-loathing, followed by some self-punishment and then I'd slowly start to feel better. However, in time I'd always let myself go right back to drinking and the cycle would repeat itself. This became my new pattern, except this time it involved ecstasy, MDMA and occasionally cocaine.

I actually had some fun times with the drugs, as I had done with the drinking. I surrendered to the party scene and joined in with taking an E at the beginning of the night to get the evening going and doing a few lines of coke throughout if there was some on offer. I often talked a lot and when I was on drugs, I didn't get tired at all. I was so awake and would want to stay up chatting away with whoever else also couldn't sleep. I felt connected and loved from within and with everyone else, there was no small talk, we could get right to the deep stuff that I craved, and I didn't want that feeling to end. So, I'd keep going. I was frequently one of the last ones standing and I'd still be up talking well into the morning hours. There was one time when I, with a few others, was kicked out of the person's home at one in the afternoon after being there the whole night before!

If someone was offering me cocaine, I found it really hard to say no and there were even a couple of times when I did it during the week, then went to work having not slept. I'd be still buzzing, trying to hold it together, but usually crashing big majorly around lunchtime.

After nights like these I'd feel so exhausted that when I was able to sleep, I'd be out for at least 12 hours, that was always a relief – another escape from it all.

These nights would then alternate with the 'come downs'. And for me, they were bad! I would feel almost suicidal on these days. It felt similar to my university days.

But I craved connection and wanting to be loved. So, I did what I knew how, I looked outside and joined a number of dating websites. In the beginning it was fun and quite harmless, I had fun chatting to guys online and went on a few really bad dates, but they definitely provided some amusement amongst my social circle. I think my first one was an ex-con as he had no address and was quite cagey about what he'd been up to for the past few years! I had a couple others, seemingly sweet guys at first, but they always seemed to get weird and bring the topic to sex. I swiftly left or had a friend call and give the worst excuses. It was another distraction.

But, as this continued, and over time the more into it I got, I started to realise that all the men on these sites wanted the same thing. I realise looking back now that the more sucked in I got I began to lose touch with what I wanted – which was genuine love – and I thought that the only way forward was to give these guys what they wanted. So, I obliged. With one I began sending naked photos of myself, in an effort to start a connection. I did what I was asked, even though I felt quite unsure about it.

It feels like that period is a blur of allowing too many men full control over me. I slept with men I don't even remember and was always left feeling violated and even more lonely; sad and ashamed that I had given a part of myself that I didn't even really know. A part of me that I only later learned to recognise as sacred. I'd pretend I was cool with it, that it was what I wanted, but deep down I just wanted to feel loved. There was even one occasion where I agreed to try out something with a guy and I ended up in A&E needing internal stitches! I was wiped out for a couple of weeks after that, feeling so low, embarrassed and humiliated. What was I becoming? What was I doing with my life?

It felt like such a dark time. I was all over the place, still dabbling with drugs, going to house parties, dating, broke as hell (it's amazing how you can still party and do drugs with such little money) and desperately trying to do a job I hated to pay the bills. It was all so depressing, and it wasn't me. It was like something outside of me had control of my life and I felt utterly lost and desperate inside. There were a number of times I felt like ending my life. I even took a few painkillers one evening but then decided to throw them up. I didn't know how I was going to find a way out of this, but I knew I had to.

I remember one day waking up with an awful hangover, worse than normal. I was vomiting for most of the day, unable to even keep water down, as my body couldn't take the cocktail of alcohol and drugs, I was putting in it. I called my sister in Kenya almost maniacally in tears saying I couldn't do this anymore. I was beyond 'trying' to hold it together. I was a complete mess. I was so tired of feeling like this. So tired of hating my life. Hating the body I was in. Hating everything about myself.

Things had to change

With all the things that I did to myself over the years – the self-harming, the numbing, days spent vomiting in the bathroom as my body tried to purge last night's alcohol, the accidents from nights out drinking (not always caused by me, but not helped by me either) I have fallen in the shower, fallen head first on to the pavement, lost a toe nail, had stitches in my foot, had bruises covering large parts of my body and more, the daily debilitating diarrhoea, ending up in A&E a few times – I wonder why I didn't turn my life around sooner.

The fact was I didn't care about myself. I didn't know how to care about myself. I thought it was selfish to care about myself. I didn't feel I deserved love or change. I was also addicted to escaping and numbing any feelings I had. The world was a painful place and I didn't want to feel it in any part of my being.

Even now it makes me sad thinking about the point I had got to and what I accepted and thought I deserved as my reality.

I didn't really know how to get out of the life I had created for myself. I felt trapped and powerless to change it. When I ate well and exercised, I would notice some changes – I would start to feel a bit better, perhaps drop a couple of kilos and there would be a glimmer of hope in the distance. Maybe I did like myself a bit, maybe there was hope things could change... But then as soon as this feeling came I would self-sabotage and go right back to drinking and partying, the light would fade, and I'd be back in the vicious cycle I had created for myself.

It was only when someone I love dearly got a life-threatening illness and wasn't given long to live that something in me clicked. I remember standing in my kitchen in tears after I found out feeling helpless, desperate, scared and sick. It felt all too familiar to my mum and a part of me couldn't believe I was in this place again. It was also a bit of a wake-up call as deep down I knew the way I was treating myself couldn't lead to anything positive, neither could I be of any support to anyone feeling the way I did most days.

I remember crying out – asking for help, not sure who or what I was talking to at the time. My intuition, which I had been ignoring and numbing for so long, told me that in order to help I needed to heal myself. I couldn't be there for my brother in the self-destructing downward spiral I was in.

The message I was getting and wrote down at the time was:

Forgive yourself, you deserve love and happiness. Stop sabotaging yourself every time something good happens or you make progress in life. You are here today to help and serve others, but you have to serve and help yourself first, by forgiving yourself. Let go of the past – you can't change it. Why would you want to? It has made you who you are today. Feeling guilty and beating yourself up for things that happened will not help anyone, least of all you. You deserve love. All kinds of love. Especially everlasting love from yourself. Show yourself love, treat yourself the way you have always been treating others. The way you treat people you admire and respect. Show yourself that unconditional, unwavering love that you have always longed for. Start today.

This seemed totally counterintuitive, but the feeling was so strong, and I so badly wanted to help that this is what I started to do. I stopped drinking (again) the following weekend and cut out all processed foods, I even signed up for a yoga class trial membership, which I had been meaning to do for years, having taken a few classes years ago and loving it! Instinctively I knew that to begin with I'd need to have things where I paid and would be committed particularly as I wasn't in a good place financially, and therefore likely to back out and go out drinking instead.

I was also beyond sick and tired of being the person I had

41

become. I was exhausted of all the yo-yoing between self-destruction and taking care of myself. But also, the thought of losing someone else was terrifying and that fuelled my want to change more than anything. It was such a strange feeling; it was as though if I looked after myself it would all be okay. It felt like there was a bigger force than just me trying to make change alone.

I continued with the healthy diet and yoga for two months, which was the longest amount of time I'd ever looked after myself. This is when things really started to shift on a deeper level than ever before.

My energy levels increased, and I found I didn't feel so exhausted being around London. My digestive issues which were still there (although not as bad as they had been) started to go. I felt less anxious. I found I had time and energy to read more and spent hours poring over wellness articles to feel even more inspired. I slept better, actually needing less sleep than ever before. I began to write and journal, something I'd been talking about for years but wasn't actually doing. I began to think that maybe I wasn't such an awful human being after all, maybe I was worth more than the little I'd thought of myself for so long. Maybe I was worth more time and effort. I found that exciting work and collaboration opportunities started to come to me. I met people into the same things as me almost by chance. I started to feel more and more confident (without the booze). Life just felt so much better on the inside!

I stopped feeling like I was missing out and started to tune into what my body and mind wanted and how I was feeling. It was all very new to me. I found the confidence to do a free two-day life coaching event, something I never would have done with my whole weekend when I was drinking, and eventually signed up for another course which started me on my path to where I am today.

Since then I have been through phases of reverting to old habits and self-sabotaging, but never to the extent where I was at for so many years before. That first time of really beginning to care about myself set me on a new path with new opportunities and doors opening, which meant each time I fell back into an old pattern I pulled myself out of it faster. I also recognised that I can't do it all on my own and have had support over the years from various coaches, healers and a therapist. Getting support is a big part of my ongoing healing journey.

As I began to change my life my world started to reflect how I was feeling. I noticed that my day-to-day flowed more easily. I felt calmer inside, less like I needed something to fill or numb me. I began to recognise how sensitive I really was to everything – food, drink, people, situations etc, and learned strategies and tools to help me honour that so I live more in harmony with who I really am.

When you start to give yourself the best and prioritise YOU, magic starts to happen in all areas of your life.

It took something outside of me for me to change my life and start to care about me. But as I began to slowly change my life, I then became my reason. As I really started to feel better inside my confidence and self-worth grew, and I was able to make positive, healthy choices because I felt I deserved them.

Also, the further I went on this self-healing journey, the more I discovered about myself and the more I have been able to shed and heal, so that I am able to embody more of me. It is a never-ending journey and one that I absolutely love to be on. With each week I feel like I am healing more and moving in the direction of who I am meant to be on this planet. Today there really is no turning back.

But it can be hard to care for yourself initially, especially if you have spent most of your life putting others or everything else first. There may be self-sabotaging patterns or behaviours that get in the way, you may not feel like you have the time or even deserve it.   What changed things for me was having a strong reason 'why' I wanted to really make lasting changes in the first place.

There could be many reasons such as for family, your children perhaps, or you may have a health concern or issue you are trying to address, you may just realise that your current way of living/being isn't working for you anymore and something HAS to change, or you may know that you are here for more and that only you can make it happen.

What can be your reason for beginning to make a change? Make sure it is something compelling, something that will keep you going. It can always change but having this 'why' is a great motivator for when you are getting started or for when you just want to say f*** it!

"You cannot heal the world until you heal yourself."
Unknown

A self-care journey

As I began the journey of coming back to me: acknowledging what I had been through, letting the pain come up to be felt and released, acting on the intuitive messages I felt to help me heal, I started to include a number of small practices, habits and behaviours, which it is my honour to now share with you.

Healing begins

To heal yourself, look inside.
Peel away the layers that have built up.
The layers you thought once protected you.
But they instead stopped you from connecting with your soul.
In each layer more and more is let go and released.
As it comes to the surface it loosens its grip and floats away.
All it takes is belief in yourself.
Inside the layers is a light that wants to shine.

PART TWO – SELF-CARE GUIDE

This part of the book includes 52 self-care stories/inspirations from my journey, which I used (and still use) to help me heal and find my way back into my body, along with prompts for you to reflect or journal on, that I hope might inspire you on your self-care journey.

There are things that are simple and that we all know, but may need a reminder of, as well as others which encourage you to go deeper into your self-care. With self-care I find that there are some foundational things which help me to feel great in myself – body, mind and soul, such as movement, meditation and eating well, then there are others I add on as and when I feel I need to, depending on what I am going through that day or week.

How you use this part of the book is totally up to you and I really encourage you to do what works for you, as this is what will help it to stick in the long run.

You might want to read all of the suggestions and stories then come back to the ones that feel the most relevant to you.

You might choose to do one a week, adding on as you go.

You may instead choose to use this section like an oracle card deck and open it up on a page at random and go with that suggestion for the day or week.

Whatever you decide will be right for you, trust yourself.

Wishing you a magical self-care journey.

1. Being an empath and highly sensitive person

Learning I am an empath and highly sensitive person was one of the best things that has happened to me and learning how to care for myself as one has helped me become more me.

I used to think there was something wrong with me when I was little and didn't enjoy being around lots of people and noise, unlike everybody else. I'd hate the fact that foods and drinks seemed to affect me so much more than others. I wondered why public transport drained me so much and think I was being weak or pathetic when I came off it feeling totally wiped, or angry, or all over the place. I felt it when others were in a bad mood and if there was tension in the office, I would feel low for the rest of the day. I couldn't (and still can't) stand small talk, so often used alcohol to help me get through it. I find it often takes a lot of my energy to do things, more than others, even if they physically don't take much time. I questioned why I was unable to handle seemingly normal day-to-day situations without feeling completely drained.

I learned how common it is for sensitive people to numb or escape and want to self-medicate with things like food, alcohol or other substances. It was like I didn't have control over how I was feeling a lot of the time.

But on the other hand, being sensitive has allowed me to empathise with others. Really feel a connection and understand what they are going through. To offer an understanding ear, to help provide solutions and see their bigger picture.

As an empath, I also often find myself going through heightened emotions and feelings in response to what's going on in the world, compared to many of my peers. I learned, and am still learning, how easily I absorb what's going on around me and how it affects me. I have to remind myself that sometimes the feelings I'm feeling aren't my own and that I need to do things to clear my energy regularly as well as ground myself. Things like meditation and visualisations, walks in nature and showers/baths. But it's actually doing the actions when I'm in the moment of feeling low, which can sometimes be hard.

Can you relate? Are you an empath? I encourage you to take a look back over your life and see if there are times when some of the following might resonate.

- As an empath you may have been described as overly sensitive.

- You often feel things more than others and can pick up on the feelings and emotions of others as if they were your own.

- Your energy levels can suddenly go up and down depending on what's going on around you, or more dramatically than others in accordance with the moon cycles and yearly seasons.

- You can often sense what a person is like without even knowing them. - You find it difficult to say no to others and may find you put others' needs before your own.

- You may find it easy to overeat – as you use food to help ground you or build you up when you feel low and aren't even sure why.

- Food and drinks affect you more than others - especially stimulants, highly processed or sugary items.

- The news easily affects you and you can feel sad, frustrated or angry at the state of the world. - You're generally (although not always) quite introverted and need a lot of time alone to recharge.

- You feel at your best in nature and/or with a few close friends with whom you can fully be yourself.

As an empath self-care is so important as it helps with energy levels, not feeling so drained, respecting boundaries, learning to do what's best for your body, mind and soul – and so much more!

It was such a relief learning I am a highly sensitive, introverted empath! Finally, I don't feel so alone. There are other super sensitive and empathic people out there. All the times I thought I needed to be tougher and felt frustrated at my apparent weakness, were futile. I could start to accept and love myself that little bit more.

How can you support yourself more as an empath?

I have a free Facebook group 'Self-care for empaths', which

might be of interest.

If you are a fellow empath, I have a little message for you.

The world needs you, in all your empathic beauty, to help it heal.

Yes, it is painful to feel the hurt and sadness that others' experience, not knowing how to process it. Yes, we can absorb negativity and feel emotionally drained at times, which may lead to self-destructive behaviours or numbing to avoid this. We may feel completely misunderstood and that we're alone in all that we experience. It may feel overwhelming, like there is no hope and that there is just too much suffering out there.

BUT there is so much you can give to the world by being you: by feeling all that you do; by being able to relate so strongly to others; by being the sensitive soul that you are. You can use this to offer great compassion, understanding, comfort, healing and kindness. You understand that one person's pain is everyone else's. You know that for us to all thrive we have to be there to support and help one another, we can't continue living in the paradigm of 'me' versus "us". For the world to truly heal we have to see the love in each other even in the darkest moments. You, as an empath, have this gift within you. Let your sensitivity be your super-power and embrace all the magic that it can offer the world.

Reach out to fellow empaths, ask for help, be clearer on your boundaries and put your needs first. You can then come from a place of being filled up and will have soooo much to offer this world, just by being YOU. Share your experiences of being an empath, reach out, allow yourself to be vulnerable, as you heal yourself you will heal the world around you.

 Now more than ever the world needs your empathic gifts to help it heal, but you must look after yourself first.

Love to you all.

2. It's the small things that lead to the biggest overall changes

I tried for so long to change the things I didn't like about myself and my life with a drastic 'all or nothing' approach. I found it impossible to make small changes or find any kind of maintainable balance in the different areas of my life.

I'd be the last one standing at a night out, drinking lots – often encouraging more and not wanting the night to end. Or I would be tee-total and being super strict on the latest diet I decided to embrace whether it was juicing, paleo or macrobiotic.

While working as a freelancer, I'd do long hours packing in as many different jobs as possible with no breaks, then I would completely neglect work, even having to call in sick on occasion and just rest and not want to do anything, see or even speak to anyone for a few days.

When it came to my love life, I'd go through periods of trying to find a relationship by spending hours on dating apps and going on as many dates as possible, then I'd delete all my apps and not want to see another guy for months.

I was doing what I thought I 'should' be doing. Not paying attention to what my needs were or what might work for ME.

It's only when I stopped doing this and started to make just one tiny change which felt good to me, that I would continue consistently for a period of time, gradually adding to it once that became a habit, that I really noticed a difference in my life.

Things I wanted to make happen actually started to happen, and change became something I was capable of!

I find that if we sometimes feel we aren't seeing results in a few days or weeks that nothing is happening and there's no point in continuing. I especially think this is the case in our fast-paced world of instant gratification. Learning to be patient and make small changes is so simple, yet so powerful and one we all could do with re-learning. Particularly as a sensitive being, having too much going on can be overwhelming.

Where in your life can you take it in small steps?

3. Acceptance

The sooner you accept yourself as you are, the sooner you can make changes. It seems counter-intuitive, accepting yourself to change yourself. But when you meet yourself at a place of understanding, calmness and acceptance for who you are and where you are at, you can then begin to make genuine, lasting changes towards who you truly can be.

I grew up in this idyllic situation and honestly was given everything on the outside. I knew how privileged I was and for most of my adult life I felt so guilty for having so much in comparison to others. Because of that I often felt like 'who was I to have any issues and feel anything but privileged and happy?'

It took me a long time to accept that I was allowed to not feel that; that it was okay to not feel okay; that there was more to me than just what appeared on the outside. That I was actually in pain on the inside and harming myself in many ways as a result. This then allowed me to really begin my healing journey.

What do you need to accept about yourself today?

4. Following the joy and the Joy of Missing Out (JOMO)

One of the first changes I made was to look for work opportunities in areas I was passionate about: cooking, health, wellness and food businesses with a sustainable edge. I spent hours scrolling through social media to find companies whose ethos and focus were in these areas. I found loads, which excited me, and I speculatively approached these businesses and, after a lot of rejection, ended up working with some of them for years as a freelancer.

This little change made me realise that actually I could start to shape my reality. Having a full-time job wasn't the only option. I began to do a number of different things beginning a portfolio career with various part time jobs in marketing, PR and admin assistance, occasional help at a supper club, lots of market research jobs, and alongside I studied more in health and wellness. It was super busy, but it was varied, and I thrived on the different projects for a while.

I also started feeling less like I was missing out on things I didn't go to. As my schedule was so busy, I had to say no to a lot. But I eventually realised I didn't want to be doing those things, and it was great to have a valid excuse. Many of them actually depleted me and I needed to keep my energy levels high. Plus, following what brought me joy and experimenting with different roles was much more exhilarating. Even though, I definitely filled my life up with too many different things (and I learned that later) I felt like I was heading in a direction that spoke to my heart at last.

What areas in your life are not bringing you joy, and you'd much rather be missing out on?

Where can you make little changes to follow or find the things that will bring you joy?

5. Movement

For years I felt like I should be going to the gym as that's what people mainly do in London (or at least that's what I thought). And I eventually did. I have had some great times in the gym and some awesome trainers who supported me, but in all honesty, the gym wasn't for me. I would feel good after going, as the endorphins rushed around my body, but then they would stop and I'd find myself eating to get a rush again, also I'd feel I 'deserved' it after my workout.

Yoga changed that for me. Yoga helped me to develop a relationship with my body and begin to look after it on a deeper level.

Also, I found I loved long walks. I'd spend hours walking around London on my own getting to know the city. These days I take long walks in nature on my own. I find walking helps me to clear my head of all the millions of thoughts I have, or even process things if I need, and I always feel so calm and connected afterwards. I'll even have catch up calls with friends while I walk, which works well too.

Movement is such a great way to get out of your head and into your body. It's a wonderful way to release emotions (whether they're your own or others'), excess energy, feelings and much more.

What movement do YOU enjoy? How can you fit it into your life so that it works for you? Or perhaps you do a lot of movement already and it might be time to try something new?

6. Nature

When I first moved to London one of the main things that I noticed was the lack of nature everywhere. Yes, London is beautiful and has wonderful green spaces and parks, but it's not quite the same as the abundance of plant life in Kenya that I was used to. It was a shock to my system, and I noticed myself begin to feel more and more trapped in the maze of concrete buildings everywhere. Given it was almost winter when I moved to the UK and my tropical bones were finding it freeeezing I didn't make the effort to get out much and find spots in nature either!

As spending barely any time in nature became my new norm, I realised how much I missed it. I craved seeing colour everywhere and wanted so badly to be walking around barefoot on the grass. I missed the ocean and smells of damp earth, rich, luscious foliage and tropical fruits.

I recognised how much better I would feel being in nature, so over time I got used to wrapping up warmly in the winter and began to make it a priority to find nature spots. I also began to accumulate quite a few house plants in my bedroom – bringing nature to me.

These days I make sure to get into nature daily (in all seasons), even if it's just for a few minutes. The effects of nature really soothe and nurture my soul.

Spending time in nature is good for everyone but seems to be particularly powerful for sensitive people as it quiets stressed and busy minds and helps to calm and ground our energy.

How can you bring more nature into your life?

7. Fresh, real food

I think we all know the benefits of eating healthy. I certainly felt them in-between my binges, as they brought me back to me.

When I first began making changes that lasted, rather than cutting out everything 'bad' in my diet, I instead increased my fresh food, so I didn't feel deprived. Then when my body got used to this, I found I wanted healthier foods and less of the things that didn't make me feel good – so was able to cut them out with ease.

Paying attention to how food makes you feel is a great way to get back in tune with nourishing yourself, and what makes you feel good.

Try and pay attention to what you are putting into your body and how it makes you feel afterwards; then increase the amount of fresh produce you are consuming and notice any changes in your mood, energy levels and how you feel overall etc.

Fresh, real food is full of life and energy and that in turn gives the body what it needs to function optimally, so you are better able to handle all that life brings. Also increasing your intake of 'juicy' fruits such as melons, pineapple, apples or citrus and savoury fruits like tomatoes and cucumbers is incredibly hydrating. Try it out and see how it works for you.

What you put into your body will have an effect on all areas of your life.

Are you nourishing your body with a variety of raw and cooked fresh produce?

How can you increase the amount of fresh fruit and veg you eat on a daily basis?

8. Be bad

So much of life is spent pleasing others or feeling like you have to do the so-called 'right', 'good' or 'perfect' thing. I did this with my all or nothing approach. Being 'good', following strict diets, being a certain way, doing what I thought was right, when there was a part inside of me who wanted to be 'bad', and just say f*** it and do things I wasn't 'supposed' to as I get bored being 'good' all the time!

Instead, when I honour the 'bad' part of myself and let her come out to play by paying more attention to her needs as they arise, she comes out in a much gentler way. Not in the extreme way from when I shut her away and she would explode out of me as she 'had' to come out!

It's so liberating, freeing and an affirmation that I genuinely care about my varying needs!

How can you be 'bad' without hurting yourself or anyone else?

Goodbye good girl

I'm SO fed up of being the good girl
The girl who does the 'right' thing.
The girl that doesn't get angry.
The girt that does what she's told.
The girl who puts everyone else first.
The girl who would never dream of being honest if it meant
hurting someone else's feelings.
The girl who smiles even when she feels shit inside.

The girl who puts on a brave face no matter what.
The girl who has forgotten what it feels like to 'feel' in case it
stirs up something.
The girl who would never dream of being bad.
I am SO fed up of being her.
She served her purpose, I'm grateful to her for protecting me,
for doing what she thought was best. But now it's time to say
farewell.
This is it. I am done.
Goodbye Good Girl.
Goodbye.

9. **Stop apologising**

I used to apologise for everything I did, even just for answering a question. If someone asked me what I wanted to do, I would say 'I'd like to do xxx, I'm sorry.' If I needed anything I would start with 'I'm sorry but xxx".

I would apologise for having an opinion.

For wanting, or not wanting something.

Even for taking up space.

The list goes on.

It was like I felt I had to apologise for being me.

If I was ever going to be happy with myself, I had to stop apologising for being myself!

So, over time I consciously became more aware of when I did this and stopped myself. Today I only apologise if something is genuinely my fault.

Is there anywhere in your life where you apologise for no reason?

10. People-pleasing

I people-pleased for years, to keep the peace more than anything. I hated turmoil and upset and found it much easier to do what I 'thought' others wanted, rather than go with what I wanted. I was so concerned with keeping everyone else calm and happy, what I wanted became a distant memory and I lost my connection to what that even was.

I found myself feeling so exhausted by doing things I thought others wanted and always putting myself last to make sure I wasn't disapproved of.

It wasn't easy to stop this, but over time I started saying 'no' more. I re-learned how to check in with myself and know what I wanted, paying attention to how my body felt when faced with a choice, then I began to honour that feeling.

I also began to look at areas in my life where I was over-giving and always available. Being the eldest I'd learned to be the helpful one, and always be there to look after the younger ones, which served me for a time. I realised I had to put my needs first or I wouldn't ever be the person I wanted to be inside.

As I started to do this, I found I had more energy and eventually many of the things I didn't even want to do stopped appearing in my life.

Do you find you people-please?

Perhaps you do it because you want to keep the peace? Maybe

you're worried about how someone else might react? You could fear you'll be rejected if you don't please others? Or maybe you feel what others' feel and want to make sure their needs are met even if it comes at the expense of your own?

It could be any or all of these things. Either way, people-pleasing will leave you feeling depleted in the long run and unsure of who you authentically are. It's a wonderful thing wanting to help and be there for others, but not if it goes against your needs.

I encourage you to think about any areas in your life where you might be people-pleasing. How can you start to change this?

11.   Gratitude

People are always going on about the benefits of gratitude and keeping a gratitude journal etc., and I can tell you this one thing has probably single-handedly helped me change my life.

When you are trying to find things to be thankful for in even the darkest moments – things like having a roof over your head, being able to read this page, having food and water – some of the basic things we take for total granted, will help you to turn your perspective right around.

Even in moments when I was struggling and saw no way out, for example when I had no job or money for rent and thought I'd be homeless, coming back to gratitude was so powerful and helped me move beyond my desperation and acknowledge how much I still had.

Gratitude has helped me to change my perspective and look at my life, my past, all that has happened and see it as something that has happened FOR me, rather than TO me.

Can you list 20 things you are grateful for right now?

12.   De-cluttering

For years I accumulated 'stuff'. I used shopping as another way to make myself feel better. I had even become a bit of a hoarder, holding on to things for 'one day' or because I felt if I got rid of them, they would take away a part of me or my memories.

But deep down I actually felt quite overwhelmed by all I had. Also living in London and moving nine times in 12 years, each time with more stuff, and much in the same boxes from the last move, was getting tiring!

I knew I needed to do a big clear out.

I got rid of items I had bought throughout my twenties when I was working full time, that I thought would make me feel a certain way. Items that I thought made me feel whole. Items that reminded me of times in my life, but in all honesty, I didn't care that much about.

I had countless tops I'd only wore once on a night out. Clothes with the tags still on, at least two to three sizes smaller than I was, which I was saving for 'that day' when I was going to be slim enough to fit into them. I had bags of jewellery and shoes as these two things made me feel better (momentarily) even with my fluctuating weight.

I ended up with about 10 large bin bags full of stuff! Giving it all away felt so light and free-ing and definitely helped me with releasing my emotional attachment to things.

I have a new rule today, every time I bring in something new, I have to also get rid of or give something away in its place, and I'm now moving more towards being a minimalist frequently getting rid of more things, as it suits me. I love the feeling of not having much stuff.

Having an excess of 'things' and 'stuff' can also be quite overwhelming for an empath as there is often a lot of emotional energy associated with the items that you can literally feel.

Where do you need to de-clutter in your physical space?

13. Letting go

As I began to de-clutter my physical surroundings, I also started to let go of things that were holding me back or not serving me. Attachments to ways of thinking or being that I thought were a part of me. Other people's thoughts and ideas that I thought were the only way.

I used to have very fixed ideas on how I wanted things to be and try and control the outcomes. I tried to control me, my shape, what I ate, everything.

Loosening my 'control' here and eventually letting go of it has helped me relax more into myself and means I don't feel so anxious all the time. This has probably been one of the hardest things for me and I still find some days when I want to control everything, when I'm holding on tightly to an outcome... But reminding myself it's actually not possible to control everything again and again, and again, is what I keep coming back to, and over time it gets easier to 'let go'.

This area, in itself, is huge and the more and more I let go, the more I realise there is to let go of.

What can you let go of that is no longer serving you? What are you holding on to that it is time to let go of? It could be things, habits, behaviours, certain situations, people even...

14.   Play and have fun

I don't think this self-care journey would be quite as appealing if it wasn't also fun.

I feel like so many of us have forgotten how to play and have fun, at least in the carefree, belly aching from so much laughter, kind of way that children often do.

When I began to find the fun in things that weren't also harmful to me, I remembered how much I loved to move my body. I intuitively decided to sign up for Zumba classes, for a change to my yoga ones, and found I had so much fun. I was able to loosen up and laugh at myself as I got the steps totally wrong.

What do you do for play and fun? Is there something new you want to try?

15. Breathing

So simple, yet so profound. We do it naturally of course, but so often we don't breathe fully into our entire being. Yoga and meditation helped me with this.

Taking time to breathe deeply is an essential part of my self-care today. In between calls, clients, things on my to-do list. Taking regular moments throughout my day to connect with my breath and give my entire body fresh air is calming, restorative, stress-busting and grounding.

Something I particularly like to do these days is place one or both hands on to my heart or my lower belly and breathe into this space. With each in breath I imagine love filling it up.

Do you take the time to stop and breathe deeply? Try it, especially in moments where you maybe feel overwhelmed, anxious or disconnected.

16. Creating space

The spaces of seeming nothingness in our lives are so important as they allow our minds and bodies to absorb, assimilate and do what they need to. We live in a world where being busy is seen to be the only way to be productive, but there is so much magic to be found in the spaces in between.

Have you ever noticed that you get your best ideas after sleep, or doing something unrelated to what you 'needed' to be doing? Perhaps you remember something important after chilling out.

This is an ongoing one for me as for many years I've tried to fill up the spaces in my life (in my body and time) with food, drinking, shopping, TV etc.

I am still learning to sit with the space and not find something to 'do'. I'm learning to listen to my body and not try to fill it with food, even when it's not hungry.

By doing this I find I am able to sink deeper into who I really am.

I need space....

Space physically, in my surroundings.
Space to connect with myself.
Space to connect with others.
Space to connect with nature.
Space to hear my inner guidance.
Space to tell what's mine and what's not.
Space to rest and replenish.

Space to allow.
Space to be present.
Space to just be.

Where do you try to fill the spaces in your life?
How can you create more space in your life?

17.   Comparing myself to others

For so long I'd look to others and what I thought I wanted to be/do/feel as a measure of how 'well' I was doing. If I wasn't where they were, I wasn't 'there'. I thought that if I had what they had or if I looked like them, I would be complete.

Living and working in central London didn't help. I was inundated with media messages of how to look and if I just bought this item or did this thing, I would be happy. My young, malleable mind was hooked, and I spent a lot of money on things to feel better about myself.

I also felt the pressure to be a certain way. It was weird that I didn't know what I wanted, and I had friends who thought we should be getting married, having children and buying a house, at our age. I SO didn't feel that though. I felt I still needed to go through stuff. Still needed to shed layers. Learn who I really was deep inside.

I'm grateful to my dad, as he always said that I should do life my own way. He encouraged me to follow my dreams and asked me what is 'normal'? I knew deep down inside that he was right, I felt that too. When I began to follow my own path, he supported me and always just allowed me to be me.

Really getting to know myself and appreciate myself for being me was life changing and helped me melt further into my own being. I wouldn't be where I am today if I had done what I thought I 'should' do!

Do you ever compare yourself to others?

Social media can be a prime place for this — I still find myself comparing my life to others' 'highlights' on their feeds.

Look out for this and try not to compare, instead you could perhaps notice what moves you in others and let it inspire you. I often find when I compare myself to others it's because I want what that person has, so I know it is something to move towards in my own life.

Also remember you are uniquely beautiful because you are YOU. This is your life and your journey. Celebrate your individuality and applaud others when they embrace theirs.

18.   Creativity

We are ALL creative beings. Fact.

By holding our creativity back, we are doing ourselves and the world a disservice.

I truly believe that by expressing ourselves creatively we are honouring our own self-care and in doing so we heal ourselves and the world around us.

I know from personal experience what a relief I feel when I create. I grew up loving art, cooking, acting and making things. In school, art classes were one of my releases, my sanctuary for me to escape from my difficult home life. Nature was my muse and when I was left alone with my pencils, pastels and a blank sheet of paper, hours would pass by and I would feel so free, and like I could just be me. I loved the freedom and excitement from not knowing what might come out of me, what might take shape on the paper in front of me. I even went so far as to do an art degree, which I thought would further my creativity.

Sadly, for me, I found I had to do art a certain way, which went against what I wanted to do. A way that fit into what society demanded – it had to be art that could make a career. I was told I wasn't good, and I even failed my art degree the first time I did it. It ruined art for me, and it was over 14 years until (with the support of some incredible friends) I picked up a pencil and paintbrush for the first time.

When I did, I remembered just how much I love to create. To

express... To allow... To put colour on paper. From then it has snowballed, and I finally have the confidence to begin creating again.

The difference? This time it's for ME!

When I walked into an art store for the first time in years, I honestly felt like a kid in a candy shop – the colours, the materials, the textures – so much beauty, so much possibility. It just made my soul SO happy. This is the ultimate form of self-care for me!

Getting creative in a way that works for you (it could be painting, flower arranging, cooking, photography, dancing – anything that allows YOU to express yourself) is such a good way to release emotions, get into the flow and reconnect with yourself.

I encourage you to do something creative that's just for YOU. What do you enjoy creating? If you aren't sure perhaps think back to what you loved doing as a child – that may spark some ideas.

19. Technology

I love how technology connects us. I am able to work entirely from my laptop and have found my soul family through online groups, programmes and interactions. Also having my own family all over the world means I can connect with them when I want.

I remember when I first moved to the UK. I would have to buy phone cards which gave me a good rate to Kenya, and I'd use the phone box outside the halls of residence to make crackled, barely audible calls to my family once a week. If we had the technology that we do today, then I might not have felt so homesick and disconnected.

Technology truly is a blessing in many ways, but it's also incredibly hard on us as human beings, and particularly sensitive people. Amongst some of the things like repetitive strain injury from too much use, and bad eyesight, it really doesn't serve us to be on it all the time. I find I feel really wired, tired and dehydrated after too much laptop use. Also, I have noticed I get addicted to checking things like my Instagram – there are times when my hand reaches over to pick up my phone constantly throughout the day unless I stop myself. It's almost like it sucks me in and I lose control over who I am and what I need.

Taking a digital detox

How much time do you spend immersed in the digital world, be it surfing the web, on your phone, on social media sites, watching videos online? Be honest with yourself.

Tech can have a really negative influence on us in that it not only affects us physically, it also leads to comparing yourself to others' highlights on social media. Let's be honest, we tend to share more of our 'good' moments than our messy ones. This can leave you feeling 'less than', or 'not good enough' and totally disconnected from reality. It certainly does this to me at times.

I encourage you to take a digital detox that works for you. This may mean you take a few hours off each day, perhaps you detox from tech one whole day a week, or maybe it's just turning off all your devices half an hour before you go to bed. Do what is right for you and where you are at.

20. Free-writing

I used to have one of those minds that is all over the place and literally never stops – a monkey mind, if you will. From the minute I woke up, it was thoughts and questions, consistently chattering away – observing, asking, analysing, over-analysing, repeating, remembering etc. It was exhausting.

I want to share a tool that I have been using on and off for the last few years now, which has helped transform the way I go through my days (amongst other things). It is an awesome practice called Morning Pages, and comes from a beautiful book by Julia Cameron, called The Artist's Way.

Morning Pages is something you do as soon as you wake up, before doing anything else which requires considered brain power (so a trip to the toilet and a drink are fine, but definitely NO checking phones or emails). What you do is by hand free-write down all the thoughts going through your head on to three pages (I use an A4 notepad).

You're probably thinking how on earth am I going to write three pages? I did when I started, but trust me, if you have a mind full of thoughts it just starts to flow, and you'll be amazed at how fast it goes.

You literally just 'brain dump' all the thoughts running around and don't stop until you are finished. Mine have varied from starting writing about how tired and grumpy I am, to how beautiful the weather is, to analysing scenarios or situations, to feelings that are coming up, to what my dreams were, things

I'm grateful for, to thoughts about what I was going to eat, to how excited I am about something. It totally varies each day. The idea is to get all of those things out of your head, as they are better out than in, so you can unlock the good stuff – the creativity and interesting ideas, which will help you get on with your day in an awesome way.

More recently as I have less 'clutter' which needs to come out I can also ask myself questions which will help me connect with myself and help me figure out things I want to do.

It does mean getting up a bit earlier but trust me you won't regret it.

If mornings really aren't an option for you – try doing the activity at another time of the day that works for you.

Where can you put some time aside to free-write, or wake up early and do morning pages?

21.   Finding the magic

When I was little, I believed in magic. I used to make magic potions out of flower petals I'd find in the garden, mixed with food extracts from the kitchen and anything else I could find that I thought would fit. I would cast spells and pretend that anything I touched would turn to gold, or if I wanted to, I could make myself invisible. I fully believed in fairies at the bottom of the school playing fields and at night time I just knew there were angels around. I would sometimes talk to them and felt they were there protecting me. Being a child, was for me, a truly magical experience for the most part. When I was left alone, I believed anything was possible. I'd set out fearlessly on mini adventures around our jungle-like garden in Kenya – I'd gather different types of tropical flowers for creations and adornments; I would pretend I was a mermaid and swim for hours in our little pool; I felt totally safe and the world was my magical kingdom, to be, do and have whatever I believed in. As I grew up and life 'happened', I stopped believing in this magical place. Instead I started to numb and escape my reality in other ways that were harmful.

But, throughout all of these experiences since I brushed the magic world away, there's always been that little girl inside who DID still believe. There was this buried feeling that something was missing, that there had to be more to life than what's on the surface, than what we experience physically. Throughout my teens and twenties I was fascinated by anything 'new-agey' and had a little stash of crystals, incense and some books which were considered weird by many. I remember being drawn to friends, particularly older women who had a bit of a hippy, alternative lifestyle. In particular, one friend who introduced me to meditation when I was 19 and got me sessions with a reiki practitioner and psychic, which I found fascinating and so helpful. But, still I would never admit to being 'into' these things. It's over the past few years as I've kept on with my self-care path and doing more of the things that make me happy (particularly through reading widely in a number of self-development areas), I started to come across others who also believed in magic, or at least the same kind of magic that I did, and as I later came to know it – the spiritual world or the metaphysical. The spiritual world has been like a candy shop for my inner child. All the different tools and practices you can play with such as: Angel and oracle cards for that little bit of extra guidance, energy healings and clearings, tapping into the potency of moon cycles and the earth's changing seasons, astrology, meditation, and so much more.

These are just a few of the tools and practices I've experimented with and it has been so much fun and totally magical. But, and this is the BUT, the real thing they've done, alongside lots of other self-care practices, is help ME to find ME. They've helped me to unlock the real me hiding beneath all the layers. They've helped me to connect with my true self inside so I can show up more in the world, express what I want to express and do more of what my heart truly desires. They've helped me to come home to myself. My life has honestly changed since I've allowed myself to believe in the magic once again.

I guess the real magic is believing in myself.

Magical moments

I encourage you to notice the magical moments that happen around you or in your life.

Maybe it's the sunlight flickering through the trees; a spontaneous kiss; a mouth-wateringly delicious meal; a gorgeous sunset; a bus arriving as soon as you get to the bus stop, and you getting a seat right where you want; a moment of synchronicity – the list is endless.

The more you notice and appreciate these little things which make you happy, the more they will appear.

Where's the magic in your life?

22.   Treat yourself

An important part of my self-care journey was making sure to treat myself while I made changes in my life. It meant I didn't feel like I was depriving myself in the beginning and I found it much more motivating than my previous all or nothing approach.

Over time I found I didn't need 'treats' so much as the treat was feeling so good inside myself. But it was fun to find new ways to treat myself that were within my budget and made me feel good on a deep level. This varied from things like making raw chocolate; having a bath with essential oils to getting myself fresh flowers, which made me happy.

When was the last time you treated yourself to something you really enjoy and that nourishes you? What can you do to treat yourself this week?

23. Developing a relationship with my body

I've been on over 50 diets. The first I can remember was a calorie controlled one, when I was 11 years old, which was the latest to come out of the USA and claimed you could lose up to 10 pounds in three days! My best friend's mum was doing it – so my friend and I thought it would work for us and we borrowed her book to do it secretly. We had been weighed recently in school and were slightly heavier than the other kids, and that was it – we didn't want to be!   The diet included things like grapefruit, dry toast, cottage cheese and lean protein and now when I think about it, I realise it didn't include more than around 500 calories a day. Not great for an active person, let alone a growing 11-year-old who was doing more than an hour of sport every day too.   This began my journey of trying to get my body to be smaller. I started to watch what I ate meticulously and weigh myself constantly, upset if I hadn't lost at least a couple of pounds each day. I would stand in front of the mirror and examine every part of my body wishing that certain parts were tighter, or smaller, or less round. I didn't like that my hips and bum were starting to grow!   Diets following this would be based on the first one. I knew if I stuck to a limited amount of food, I'd lose weight.

Throughout my teens and particularly my twenties I'd read voraciously on dieting and nutrition and jump on to any fad going with the promise of fast results. Deep down, I knew what to eat to feel healthy and good, but always seemed to self-sabotage or get lured into the newest 'diet'. I saw my body as something separate to me – something I wanted to control and shape, to fit in with what I thought it should be; something that rarely did what I wanted it to – I'd have to work harder and harder each year to get it to be the size and shape I thought it should be.   Things only started to change when I started to practice yoga. Yoga was different from everything else I had done. I started yoga originally for my mind as I found myself feeling anxious a lot from all the thoughts I had in my head. I was also going through a stressful, hard situation personally and remembered that yoga would help me to feel calmer, having taken some classes when I was 19 and loving them.   What happened surprised me – yoga was soft and nurturing and calmed my mind, yes, but it also started to connect me to my body in a way I had never felt before. I started to feel the strength of my legs, the muscles in my arms and back as they held me in downward dog, the flexibility of my hips slowly started to increase (as they had been quite tight for years) and I even started to feel the muscles in my bum working! I started to feel appreciation for this vessel that holds me, and wanted to nourish it so it could thrive and do more for me, with me.   I'm grateful to yoga as it helped me realise that this is my body right now, today. Starting to appreciate it and treat it with respect has led to wonderful changes physically and allowed me to feel calmer and not so controlling. It's so much better to be working with your body than against it, trust me!

How connected are you to your body? Is there something you can do to appreciate it?

24. Listening to my body

Our bodies are always sending us messages. Something that starts as a small niggle or pain, something that doesn't feel quite in check is your body's way of communicating with you that things aren't all right.

A few ways I've learned to listen to my body are by how foods and drinks affect me. I know that caffeine can give me a bit of a high, if I have more than one cup I will crash after and feel very thirsty.

For years my body was screaming at me that it wasn't okay. What started as some small stomach upsets and occasional digestive issues turned into uncontrollable diarrhoea. I also realised that meat and dairy products were making me feel sluggish and heavy, so I am now vegan (for other reasons too), but this was quite a shift from the girl who was a self-proclaimed carnivore and would eat canned sardines and biltong as snacks!

Learning to read my body's signs and signals has been a gift, and stopping and slowing down, not just reacting, has been key to this listening.

I of course still have days when I do the opposite of what my body needs, but that's okay! I learn again and remember to pay more attention as when I don't listen to my body, I usually don't feel so good later.

There is so much wisdom in our bodies.
We can learn so much from them.
They speak to us in whispers, only heard by those that really listen.
If you don't hear them, they get louder and louder,
And if you ignore them, they will scream at you.
Pay attention.
Listen.
That's all you ever have to do.
Listen.
Those tingles, tweaks, aches – they're sending you a message.
Listen.
When you do, all will be well.
Life will become magical.
You'll have a partnership unlike any relationship you've ever experienced.

Sometimes I close my eyes and feel into the different parts of my body then write the messages that come up:

Listen to me.
Feel me.
Hear me.
I need release.
I need you to listen.
If you don't, I will find ways to reach you.

All you ever need or want is inside.
Take moments of quiet and stillness,
Then you'll hear my whispers.

I will always keep you informed.
I want us to be best friends.
I want us to do this journey together.

If you listen to your body, really get to know it as you would a close friend, you'll start to see that certain types of movement/ exercise work better for you at different times. Sometimes you need hearty, warming meals whilst at other times a fresh salad is what you really want.

Living on autopilot doing what we think we should do, and not really checking in regularly to see what we need, is not living in balance and harmony with ourselves.

Give it a go, listen to your body. What does it need today? Or even this week?

25.   Passion

I lost the passion in my life for so long.

I wasn't passionate about anything (apart from food and drinking and that was in destructive way), had no sex drive whatsoever for many years, and forgot what passion even felt like.

To me passion really does mean being fully surrendered…. In my body, in my heart, connected and in tune with its different needs and sensations. I go in and out, some days it's easier to connect to my passion than others, but that's okay too.

Today I feel passionate about health and wellness and helping others.

I am passionate about always learning, growing and evolving.

I feel passionate about looking after this beautiful planet.

I get passionate about good raw chocolate.

It's a start.

What are you passionate about? Where do you need more passion in your life?

26.   Cyclical living

Growing up on the equator in Kenya, I didn't really have seasons. Moving to the UK and getting used to living with seasons was a bit of a shock to my system, especially when it was so cold and dark, and winter seemed to drag on for ages! It took me a while to realise how to care for myself and that what I needed in the summertime was totally different to what I needed in the winter.

In my early days I would try and make myself eat salads and go to the gym all year around, and then I'd get frustrated with myself when I went off-track or found it hard to stick to. I didn't realise that it was natural to feel more inward and inclined towards gentle activities during the darker colder days, whereas in the summer I'd feel much more energised.

As I started paying more attention to how I felt and what I needed throughout the year, I also started to realise the fluctuations and varying needs I felt within a month coincided with my monthly cycle. I found that one week I was totally up for going out and could get so much done in a day, and a week later all I wanted to do was spend the day indoors watching a good series.

It felt weird to have all these contrasting needs in a month and I tried to push through and ignore my body if it wanted rest, feeling guilty for wanting to take it easy at the beginning of my monthly cycle. I also felt the added societal pressure where it's seen as weak to take days off and it's almost a badge of honour to pop a painkiller and push through pain, achieve and strive even when our bodies are screaming at us to stop or slow down.

Over the years I started listening to my body honouring what it needs, so that my self-care varies throughout the month and year. There's no fixed plan and after a few years of experimenting and getting to know myself better it's much more intuitive. Of course, there are exceptions and times when I have commitments, or things I must get done but, on the whole, this is how I have adapted my self-care.

I find that in the autumn and winter seasons I want to go more inwards and need more rest and nurturing, nourishing activities. This generally corresponds to when I am pre-menstrual and menstruating in my cycle. Whereas in spring and summer I have more energy and can do more active, outward activities. This time mostly corresponds to when I have finished menstruating and am ovulating.

Having lived like this for a while and noticing the effects it has on my overall wellbeing, I really recommend taking the seasons (internal and external) into consideration when choosing what self-care actions will work best for you. There will be things that will likely feel good at all times, such as sleep, eating well and getting fresh air. However, you may notice slight variations in how you practice these actions as the seasons change. Additionally, I encourage eating seasonal foods as much as possible as you'll find they nourish you on a deeper level than having something that has been shipped halfway across the world.

We are cyclical beings and what works for one person may be totally different for another. I encourage you to start to notice how YOU feel at different times in the month and year and what activities feel good for you, in conjunction with your own cycle (if relevant). You may even notice that you feel energised and more connected overall as you work with your body and not against it.

What can you begin to do to start honouring the seasons, inner and outer? I have some resources at the end which may support you here.

27.   Making wellness my own

Wellness is a term I have had a love-hate relationship with over the years as I used to wonder, what really is wellness? Is it health? Is it looking a certain way?

In my twenties, wellness meant jumping on the various bandwagons of celebrity endorsed diets, in an effort to – 'be', 'look like', or 'feel like' how that particular celebrity appeared. I went through years of being super strict with myself as I followed a certain diet. One month it was paleo, the next was superfoods only, I tried macrobiotic, then it was raw food, then I'd cut out sugar, did juicing, counting calories, I even tried Atkins for a few days.

Following (or trying to follow) these unrealistic standards set me up for constant failure and I yo-yoed between sticking to my plan, then inevitably 'falling off the wagon', which was always accompanied by guilt and anger at myself for 'failing'. I put my body through so much and constantly chopping and changing between different diets left me feeling totally confused and like I was never getting anywhere – wherever that elusive destination was.

We all know that eating more fruits and vegetables, less processed foods and getting our bodies moving are good for our health. Aside from that there can be waaaay too many things that one feels like they 'should' be doing when it comes to health. Taking a certain number of supplements, making sure to include superfoods, cutting out meat, making sure to eat meat, avoiding sugar at all costs. Nutrition information can be a confusing and contradictory minefield and it's sometimes hard to know where to even start!

Deciding to ditch the dieting and hamster wheel of trying to fit into what I thought I should be, and starting to pay attention to what MY body needs and what my sleep, moods etc are like when I eat and drink certain things, have been some of the greatest things I've ever done for myself.

Alongside that, and something I learned when I did my health coach training (but is also intuitively so correct), was understanding (and really feeling) how much of a part the rest of our lives play when it comes to our health, NOT just food and exercise. It's the loving what you do every day, waking up and feeling happy so you don't turn to the biscuit tin or want to numb how you feel with copious amounts of booze. Having nourishing relationships, feeling like you can express yourself creatively, having space to breathe and time to connect with yourself away from others' demands. All these different factors (plus more) play a part in our overall wellness.

Learning to listen to myself and honour my evolving needs has been life changing. I now know that meat and dairy have been making me feel sluggish for years. I let myself drink alcohol when I want to (which isn't very often as I'm more connected to my feelings behind why I want to drink), and don't beat myself up like how I used to when I have a few too many! I know I need at least a day a week alone to recharge, sleep and just be. I find I get overwhelmed easily if I have too many small different things going on at once. I need to do something creative every week (for me that's cooking, writing or art) or I feel uninspired and want to fall into one of my old patterns of drinking to excess, just to create some excitement in my life.

Wellness, for me today, means accepting all parts of me, even when they aren't society's image of what wellness looks like. Yes, I'm curvy and have big hips, that's fine and I'm learning to accept my body, even love it, for what it is. Wellness includes me showing up as the real me, not afraid to not have it all figured out (who does really!), not afraid to be down some days, messy and not on form, whereas other days I feel fantastic and am bouncing off the walls with happiness.

I accept there'll be days I need distractions such as endless episodes of a show I'm into or pigging out on a delicious vegan pizza. Although I know that when I do these things I can easily spiral and these days I'm trying to be more conscious of balancing them with things that make me feel good longer term... Easier said than done, especially when I have loads going on. So, it's an ongoing journey and one that I pay attention to and adjust every week. Except this time, it's coming from a place of awareness and how it makes ME feel.

Tapping into what YOU need and what makes YOU feel good in your skin is, in my opinion, the way to wellness. Why define your wellness by someone else's standards?

What does wellness mean to you?

Something you could begin to do is start a food and mood journal, to start connecting to how certain foods make you feel, as well as noticing how different things affect you in your day-today. Tapping into these moments and un-layering the patterns, feelings and emotions behind them, alongside how foods affect you individually is the beginning of a beautiful, unique wellness journey.

28. Life is not a straight line

Some days I feel on top of the world, things are awesome, and nothing can shake the positivity and magic I feel.

Others are not quite that way, they can be messy; I feel all over the place, I'm sad, then I'm lonely, then I don't even know what I feel.

Then I just want to eat the world.

That's life. It's not a straight line. It's not going to be up, positive and upbeat all the time!

This journey can be messy.
Life is cyclical, all over the place.
When you think you're getting somewhere, something pops up
and takes you on a tangent.
It is not a straight line.
Surrender.
Allow.
Be okay with that.
You'll find that things flow more.

Where can you surrender and allow things to flow more in your life?

29. I didn't know how 'crap' I was feeling until I started to feel good.

When I started to spend more than only a few days here or there looking after myself I began to notice all the effects of the positive habits and behaviours, exercise and nutrient rich foods were having, as I was actually giving my body time to adjust and assimilate all the 'good' I had been giving it. Some of these changes were more energy, feeling happier and calmer, losing weight more effortlessly, and softer, glowing skin. Realising who I am and my strengths as a human being, as well as honouring me for being me.

I noticed how awesome I could actually feel in my body, realising that for years I'd actually been feeling bloated, tired, moody and anxious, which I had just accepted as my normal.

When you give yourself the time and dedication to look after YOU and honour what you need, you may realise also that you have been living on autopilot feeling 'less than' but accepting it as your norm.

What are you accepting in your life as 'okay', but deep down inside you know it could be sooo much better?

30.   You are whole

*Coming back to yourself is one of the greatest things you'll
ever do.
Feeling your body wholly.
Being present with all your feelings, emotions and sensations.
Knowing what it truly feels like to be you.
What makes you come alive.
What moves you.
What brings you joy.
Loving each and every part of yourself.*

*This body you have is a gift.
It carries you, supports you, heals and restores.
It's a resilient place to live.*

How can you honour yourself today so that you remember your wholeness?

31. Mothering myself

I sometimes feel like I lost two mothers, even though I barely knew the first one, the biological one, the one that carried me from conception to birth.

There's a part inside of me that feels like I know her, that we'll always be connected. It's also been so many years now since my mum passed on. Every year the memories fade, but with her too, I know I am always connected and a part of her is always with me.

When I lost my mum to cancer at eight years old, life changed pretty much overnight. Nobody can ever prepare you for something like that and you don't know how it will affect you or the other people in your life for that matter. As the eldest child, I definitely felt like I had to be the strong one, that showing emotion of any kind was weak and that if I didn't accept it, it was almost like I was ungrateful for all that I still had. It sounds weird, I know, for a child to feel like she cannot grieve, but those were the expectations I felt, whether perceived or real. So that's how I decided to live and that's when I started to build up my layers of protection, physically as well as emotionally.

With a father who was grieving and handling things in his own way, I also became a mother to my younger siblings at the age of eight. I numbed anything I was feeling, so it didn't have to be acknowledged – and I just got on with it.

What I learned much later is that I needed mothering too. The little girl inside of me needed a mother and I didn't know how to care for myself as well as handle everything else.

This part of my journey has been the hardest. Learning to mother myself. It took time, practice, baby steps. Imagining I was my own child and how I would treat her.

But over time it got easier and I made this promise:

To be gentle with myself
To care for myself
To comfort myself
To nurture myself
To soothe myself
To embrace myself
To not be so hard on myself
To allow myself to feel
To hold myself when I am sad
To be kind to myself
To love myself

Perhaps you can make your own promise to yourself?

32.   Planet Earth is also our mother

The Earth is also our mother and she has been there always. She is there to hold, comfort and provide. She is the one that connects us, nurtures and nourishes us all. She is beautiful, majestic, abundance.

When I disconnected from my body it didn't feel safe to even be here. As I've returned and allowed myself to be held by this great mother, I realise that all the love, safety and nourishment I wanted was right here all along.

These days I spend time with my head on the ground, or in meditation my heart connected to hers allowing her to fill me up, ground me, support me.

It feels so wonderful to lie directly on the grass, the earth.
It soothes me, it nurtures me, it helps bring me back to myself.
My heart slows to beat along with her pulse.
I feel the beat of the earth flowing through me – leaving
behind the busy-ness and noise that is my life.
I feel the sun on my face, it warms my skin, it softens my joints,
I relax into it and slowly we fuse together to become one.
I am one with the earth. We are one.
I feel at home.

How can you connect more with our beautiful Mother Earth?

33.   Loving the child that is inside you

So often we go through life ignoring that little being that we once were, that had to cope and put up with so much. That little being is still inside of you and needs you to remember. All that they went through, all that has made you who you are today. Sometimes that child got care and attention and what was needed. At other times that wasn't the situation and you learned to cope with what life had dealt you. We all need mothering and now that you are grown, you can take care of that little person inside. Show them love, care and attention, acknowledgment even. Just be there for that little you.

When I first started to connect with my childhood self, little me, it was really hard, and I had so many unmet needs. I invite you to connect with little you and find out what he/she needs.

One day I connected with that little girl and this is what came up:

Remember the little girl you once were? Eyes wide and sparkly, determined face, persistence in her blood. She was ready to take on the world. She didn't care what others thought about her. She knew who she was. She knew what she wanted and was on a mission to make it happen. She didn't get scared of the unknown, she in fact thought anything was possible. She knew she was invincible, a true heroine, out to conquer... Slowly over the years as you grew older, you dulled that little girl's determination, eagerness and strength. You hid it, masked it, put it on hold for another day. You felt you had to hide parts of yourself. The bits that were 'unacceptable'. The parts that were dark or shone too brightly. You didn't want to outshine another. You moulded and dimmed your light to fit convention, but now is the time to remember that little girl. Hold her, welcome her back with love and support. She is you; you are she. She and you are one.

I feel sad for the little girl inside who couldn't express how she was feeling. Who felt she had to put on a brave face and look after everyone else. She was so little and scared and alone. She didn't know what she was doing, but she did her best. I want to hold her now. Comfort her, love her.

What does 'little you' need? How can you show 'little you' more love, care and compassion? Connect with that little person and find out what he/she needs.

34.   Asking for help

Learning to reach out, ask for help and receive support from others, is an ongoing journey for me.

I feel like we're taught from a young age that it's weak to ask for help. In fact, learning to do things on your own is an important part of growing up, and then it's later seen as a fallibility to need support with things.

If you need help from others you must not have it together, you could be seen as lazy or even self-indulgent. Instead it's seen as a badge of honour to be able to juggle multiple things – work, family, a social life and have time to look after yourself – mind, body and soul!

I held it together for years. Or at least I thought I did at the time. I'd go through periods where things seemed to run smoothly, I'd feel 'on top' of everything and I'd feel a sense of accomplishment. But these times were split up by 'life' and the increasing inner battles I had with not feeling happy deep inside.

I wouldn't reach out to anyone, I just soldiered on trying to keep things going. I would promise myself I'd try harder if I fell off the diet wagon, or I would think that everyone else had it together, so I should too. I thought it was weak to ask for help and that I should be stronger when I had moments when everything got the better of me. I thought there must be something wrong with me when I felt like I was crumbling, and I didn't want anyone to think that was the case.

This ongoing battle inside me lead to me blocking it all down or numbing everything I was feeling. I'd always say I was fine; I knew how to be the strong one, I knew how to hold it together. But really, I was bursting at the seams.

Reaching out to a therapist for the first time and admitting I couldn't do it all alone was life-changing for me. My first few therapy sessions a few years back were one of the most liberating experiences I've ever had. They unlocked all these thoughts, feelings and emotions I'd been bottling down and helped me with the clarity I needed to really start shedding away some of the layers I'd built up (literally and metaphorically), and to start looking after myself.

Since then I've worked with a few coaches, mentors and healers, done multiple group courses to work through different things and today am part of a women's group for ongoing support.

For me personally, sharing and speaking about what I am going through makes it all seem so much more manageable. Life can be complicated, there's so much going on, so many demands on us, so much pressure to be, look or feel a certain way. Sometimes it's hard to get to the bottom of all the noise and figure out who you really are and what you really want. Having someone there, who perhaps has also experienced what you have, just to listen as you figure things out is so powerful and healing.

We all have different things we could use support with – paid and not paid. It could be getting a cleaner, or more help with your children, to give you some time and space for you. It may be joining a local or an online support group, asking a friend to join an exercise class with you, working with a personal trainer, therapist or coach. Whatever it is, know that it's not weak – there's something quite humbling about reaching out for help and it actually feels incredibly powerful when you do it. Plus, you'll start to notice positive changes ripple throughout your life so much faster than when you try to do it alone!

We can all be more and give so much more when we're not overwhelmed and bursting at the seams.

Where do you need support? I encourage you to reach out. You don't have to do it all alone.

Sometimes friends and people you love find it hard to accept the changes you are making, so may not be as supportive. When you are making a change, really see who supports you and perhaps don't see as much of the people who don't, even if it's just for a while. You may find support online in a forum with people going through a similar change. Or you may even want to work with a trained professional as they can help with accountability as well as support and guidance.

What are you carrying that is really weighing you down? Something that you might even be too scared to ask for help with, or not want to admit to yourself you need help with? Or is there something you could ask for help with, such as cleaning the house, to give you more time? It is not weak to receive help and does not mean you are any less capable than you think you are.

Be courageous and take the first step towards

asking.

(I'd like to add that one of my biggest, and scariest acts of self-care reaching out for help, was setting up a GoFundMe to crowdfund and help me self-publish this book. I had the email drafted for days before I got up the nerve to send it to close friends and family. When I did, I received so much support – I was quite blown away and so incredibly grateful. It really helped me feel like I don't have to do this all alone)!

35. Receiving help

Asking for help is definitely one way to help with all of the things you may have on your 'to do' list. But something I want to invite you to consider is – how do you receive help?

I used to not even ask for help as I felt that I would then be obligated to do something in return. Or I'd feel guilty for taking someone else's time/resources etc. I'd sometimes feel 'less than' or 'not enough' for having to ask for help in the first place?

Do you find it hard to receive help? Do you judge yourself in any way for receiving support?

If this is something that comes up for you perhaps it could be a good time to start re-framing it. Think how much you get from giving help to others, perhaps it's time to let others do the same for you?

Allow yourself to ask for and *receive* help with an open heart. You may find that you start to receive even more help, as you shift your perspective.

36. Give back

No matter where I was at in my journey, I always recognised the power behind giving to others. Even at my lowest points I felt better when I gave something to someone else, from my heart.

This has taken various forms for me, from donating and raising money for environmental and animal charities; paying for a random person's bus fare; giving away free coaching for people who needed it or volunteering my time in a children's art camp.

Perhaps it's being in a City where people walk by one another on the street without acknowledging one another, perhaps it's because I walked with my head looking down for so long, but something I find even more profound is in showing another human being compassion and connection. Something as simple as a smile or a compliment, offering a seat, or helping with a bag or buggy, a genuine exchange, where we each leave thinking the world isn't so bad. This makes me feel more love inside.

Where can you give back more?

37. Sharing and connecting vulnerably

Sharing openly and vulnerably with others, with whom I felt zero judgment and complete safety, has been life changing. Without it I probably wouldn't have written this book.

Not that long ago I hated being seen. I hated people looking at me and I got so, so nervous (hands shaking, huge butterflies in my belly and heart thumping – all of it) if I ever had to share anything about myself in front of others or give my opinion on something.

When I eventually took myself out of my comfort zone and began to share some of my story, the parts I felt shameful or embarrassed about, even though it was vulnerable and I felt a whole range of emotions rise, it was also so freeing. I realised we all go through similar things; we all feel vulnerable and messy, but we are all, actually, so much more alike than different. Through my sharing I don't feel alone anymore.

How often do you connect with others on a really heartfelt level? A level which leaves you feeling nourished, understood and energised?

Dare to be vulnerable, open and seen.
Share the parts of you that might seem messy.
There is so much beauty in that truth and authenticity.
We are all looking for stories we can relate to, threads that
weave us together, reminding us that we are not alone.

116

38. Looking within

For years I was looking for external validation from friends, boyfriends, colleagues, the media, anything apart from myself. I'd let other people's opinions and viewpoints cloud my own, often feeling guilty if I couldn't live up to their expectations, needs or demands.

I didn't listen to that inner voice. That inner voice that was telling me I was too tired and needed rest over a night out, because I didn't want to hurt someone else's feelings, or because I didn't want to be seen as weak or a bore. Or the inner voice that would say to not do xyz, which I'd ignore, and it later turned out to be something I wished I hadn't done.

Even the time when I had debilitating stomach pains and diarrhoea for a prolonged period of time and I didn't trust how I was feeling, self-medicating to numb the experience instead of dealing with it, when my body was clearly screaming at me there was a problem.

I always wanted to know how everyone else did things or dealt with things, rather than trusting myself. Whilst I still absolutely admire others, their viewpoints and takes on certain things and am inspired, learning to listen to myself has really helped me settle into ME and be the person I am here to be.

Ultimately you know what is best for you and nobody can tell you that. Of course, you can get support and be inspired by others, but deep down inside you really do know what you need. Giving yourself the time and space to connect to you regularly will strengthen this connection, meaning you feel fully supported from within.

Learning to listen to what my inner voice and body is telling me, to trust myself and act accordingly has been a huge part of my self-care journey.

I know we are all at different stages with this. Perhaps you may need a little reminder to get back to it. Or, you may be new to this and if that's the case here is how I first started to connect with myself, which you might find helpful.

The first thing to do is to clear your head of all the thoughts that can be there. We all do this in different ways – do what works for you. It could be meditating, movement, getting into nature, writing everything down, doing something creative... etc. Then find a quiet place where you won't be disturbed and ask yourself 'What do I need today?' and see what comes up – you may want to just listen, or you may want to write the answers down. We all have this innate wisdom that we have moved away from. Coming back to it and learning to trust yourself is such a wonderful, powerful thing.

If you are writing the answers down, sometimes holding your pen in the hand you don't normally use can help, so you don't try to logically write down an answer, it allows it to just flow.

Also, and this is super important, allow yourself to trust what comes up. Sometimes what does come up may surprise you and you may be tempted to ignore it. But, in my experience it is never wrong and will always take you on a path that will lead to growth and magic.

Try and do this as often as you can, as the more often you connect to yourself the stronger the connection gets. It may also take time to build up this trust again. As you get into the practice more, you could even make up your own questions or ask yourself about something you have going on in your own life at the moment. Have fun doing it and if nothing comes up, that's okay, you can try again another time and there are other ways to do this!

Rather than always seeking the answers from outside, I encourage you to look within.

39. Slowing down

Stopping and slowing down really allows you to assess what is important and where you are at with everything in your life. Living on the go, with the constant external noise of people, social media, the internet etc is exhausting, as well as distracting. I don't know about you, but I find I get swept up by the buzz of things I feel I should be doing, things I could be doing, things that I may not even care about.

Taking time out regularly to connect with yourself really enables you to remember what is best for you and what you need. I have now started having daily meetings with myself (my intuition), where I stop and slow down and turn off all external media, I will go for a walk in nature or I'll meditate for a few minutes if that is all I have time for.

One of the things that has come up for me in my slowing down time is how much I love to spend time alone in solitude and that I'm actually a massive introvert. I am now starting to respect this even more. I used to feel guilty, or like something was wrong with me, if I didn't want to meet up with friends and instead wanted to have lots of time to myself. I'd make excuses, saying I had to work or had something else on, when in fact I just wanted to spend time alone reading, writing, meditating, walking, or just being. I've made a conscious decision to stop this and just say 'no', guilt-free. I am a proud introvert, I need lots of time alone, it's who I am, it's what replenishes me and makes me feel whole. Accepting and allowing it is a part of my journey.

I recognise we all have different demands on us, through work, family etc, but there is always time to slow down a bit, connect with yourself and do something for you, so I would love to encourage you to do just that.

Where in your life can you slow down?

40. Comfort zones

"Outside of the comfort zone is where the magic happens."

To make lasting changes in my life and start to be the person I know I am here to be, I had to start doing things I wasn't used to. I had to try new things, stretch myself and do things that scared me a little bit.

For example to start my own business coaching and helping others I knew I had to start connecting with people who were on this wellbeing, spiritual path. And to do this I would need to go to places and network, or find groups of likeminded people online and actually interact, rather than 'lurk and like' others' posts (which I'd done for so long), or even speak up and show my face on camera. As a highly sensitive, introverted empath this certainly wasn't easy at first. It took me way out of my comfort zone and there were many times when I almost talked myself out of not going to something, cancelling or postponing for as long as possible. But I persisted and now I'm moving onto the next level of my personal comfort zone.

To create change in your life you sometimes need to get out of your comfort zone and try something new, gently moving yourself into a new area. Use your intuition to help guide you or perhaps even look at people that inspire you to help you take those first little steps into the unknown.

It might be scary at first, but you will feel amazing and so proud of yourself once you've done it.

Where are you settling into a comfortable space? Where can you stretch yourself and do just one thing that's out of your comfort zone?

41. You are worthy

What do you put up with in your life that you make excuses for, but you know deep down could be better? Perhaps it's some consistent aches and pains, which you just put down to your body getting older. Maybe it's friends who don't actually treat you that well and leave you feeling drained. Maybe it's a job where you feel unmotivated and unchallenged and you spend your time counting down the days until the weekend.

Why don't we expect more for ourselves? Why don't we strive for a life that makes us feel wonderful and thrilled to be alive from the moment we get up in the morning? Why do we settle?

Yes, I know things can happen which are not always easy and may be out of our control, but that doesn't mean we can't change the situations we have a choice over, to make them as sweet and juicy as our heart desires.

It starts with taking the first step.

A choice followed by an action.

Little by little.

If you don't make time for you, nobody else will. How you treat yourself is how others will. Show yourself you are worthy of time, care and attention and all that happens in life will begin to reflect this.

You are so worthy.

You are so deserving.

You are so loved.

Keep reminding yourself of this.

42. Feeling the feelings

I feel blah.
I feel angry.
I feel sad.
I feel emotional.
I feel all over the place.
I feel love.
I feel confused.
I feel lonely.
I feel empty.
I feel excited.
I feel fine.
I feel pissed off.
I feel happiness.
I feel weird.
I don't know what I feel.
I just feel.

That is what it is like to feel. It's not all the upbeat and happy feelings. It's not neat and in the lines. It's messy and doesn't make sense.

Feel it anyway!

I used to do anything and everything to distract myself from feeling anything that wasn't considered 'okay' or that I thought might be hard. I'd also always say I was 'fine' if anyone asked, I was worried any other response would open up a 'can of worms'. So, whenever sadness, hurt, loneliness or other not so good feelings arose, my body almost instinctively learned to numb. It shut out all feelings so that they couldn't 'hurt' me.

When I first began therapy this pattern had been so engrained that whenever we approached any topic that might bring up feelings, my entire body would numb from the neck down and my mind would become blank. It's amazing how we learn to cope with different situations and how we've programmed ourselves to not feel certain feelings.

Over time, gently, and alone to begin with, I began to journal with my feelings, letting them surface. Allowing myself to feel things in my body felt so alien to me. I found I resisted it so much, especially when it came to memories from my childhood. It wasn't easy, but it was the most healing and freeing part of all the different things I tried to help me come back to me.

It's hard opening myself up.
Cracking open the heart I've tried so long to protect.
My layers of protection, sarcasm, dismissiveness, cynicism,
emotional hardness, all carefully interwoven on top and around
each other to seal off my vulnerability.
I have to dig deep, slowly peel away the feelings I've suppressed,
and as each one comes away, with it, the emotions it's been
holding.
I feel them again.
It is like I have to re-live that exact time and experience again.
My heart hurts, tears fall freely now, I let them.
I feel my body release, tension fades from my shoulders, my
belly feels softer.
I am allowing myself to feel.
To feel something that affected me years ago, and which I didn't

let out.
I honour myself for having the courage, the willingness, to feel
everything for the first time. To feel pain, anger, resentment,
hatred even and above all empathy, compassion, caring and
love for the little girl inside me who didn't think she was allowed
to feel these things.
I comfort her now, hold her close and softly embrace that part
of me that is now willing to feel and release.

Do you allow yourself to feel your feelings? Or do you ignore or numb them and soldier on – saying you are ok when you aren't? Do you distract or numb yourself with something else as soon as you feel anything you don't want to?

It's really healthy to allow yourself to feel what you are going through (perhaps with the support of someone you trust and feel safe with), so that you can process it and allow it to pass. It can be uncomfortable to do this as we often don't want to experience feelings such as sadness, pain, anger, loneliness. It can feel like they will be too much for us to handle.

A couple of things that helped me begin to feel are journaling (I do this to process most of what I am going through these days), listening to music (sometimes dancing) and allowing myself to cry as I find that depending on what I am listening to it can help me release. I also express my feelings through art. Perhaps experiment and find something that works for you.

Allowing the feelings

As you feel your feelings, you may find that lots of old things come up. Feelings about certain situations or times in your life, which you haven't thought about in years.

The best way to describe it is like waves coming up as you peel back the layers of an onion. Sometimes the feelings can be so real you wonder if you are actually in them all over again. But, just allow them, be with them. Ask them what they are trying to tell you. Ask them what they need. They will pass on, releasing from your being.

43. Boundaries and saying 'no'

Boundaries being crossed can come up in so many areas. At work, in relationships, with friends and family...

Ultimately, it's up to us to create boundaries with others. I know how easy it is to say 'yes' to too many things or to want to people-please and end up doing things I wish I wasn't. Or there's the guilt that can come up, and who wants to feel that.

The only thing I can say is I am still 'working' on this one. It takes constant coming back to myself, checking in and asking what I really want, what I really have time for. What my priorities are – am I saying 'yes' to someone else and 'no' to myself?

I completely understand it's harder if you are a parent for example, but what I will say is, your children will never learn your boundaries nor how to assert their own if you don't model it for them now.

I also found that as I began to assert more boundaries of my own, people gradually stopped asking for so much of me and all the fretting going on in my head about having to say 'no' was unnecessary.

It may be hard at first but taking that first little step is all you need to do.

Are there any areas in your life where you may not have clear boundaries? Where perhaps you give too much of yourself? Where you are always available? Where you just can't say no? How can you begin to put some boundaries in place?

44. Grounding

Do you ever feel like all your energy is high up in your body, that you have too many thoughts, or perhaps you feel spaced out or a bit all over the place? Absorbing lots of what is going on around you as a sensitive being can be quite challenging, so grounding and bringing yourself back 'down-to-earth' is a great practice.

Think of a tree – how strong and embodied it is when it's fully grown. The higher up they grow, the deeper their roots are. We too can be more, give more and show up more, the more grounded we are.

A great way to help ground your energy is actually getting your bare skin on the ground – walk on the grass or sand if you are near a beach, lie straight on the earth, or simply put your feet on it. Close your eyes and feel your connection with the earth.

Other things you can do are hug a tree (go for it – who cares what anyone else thinks), take a walk in an area with lots of trees as they are particularly relaxing; go swimming in the ocean, a lake or river; or you could get some flowers or plants and spend some time nurturing them.

If you can't get outside or near any plants, then simply lie on the ground at home and feel the earth supporting you as you deeply breathe in and out of your whole being.

How can you spend more time grounding yourself?

45. Being present

This is something I always come back to, as someone who has spent most of her life escaping – through all my various addictions and habits. I also find it easy to wander off into thoughts about the future and past, even coming up with scenarios for my future self – playing out scenes and conversations as though they are real.

I need to keep bringing myself back, right now, to this moment. This present moment, in my body, where everything is perfect, and is all I actually have.

I completely get how easy it is to get swept up into what's going on in this crazy, old world. We're basically bombarded with messages of what's happening everywhere else, with everyone else, all the time. As an empath, this can feel like wading through a minefield of treacle, being pulled in a million directions of feelings, thoughts and emotions that we aren't even sure are ours.

But, if you do catch yourself away from the present, acknowledge what was going on and gently bring yourself back... look at your hands, look at your feet, feel the sensations inside your body, what's going on around you? What can you see? What's happening right here, right now?

Let yourself slowly sink into this present moment. Just be with it. Take a deep breath.

Be present in your body, right here, right now.

Something else I do is not watch any news or consume too much media apart from select things that I feel aligned with. This helps me to stay present in myself more. As a highly sensitive being this may resonate with you too.

46. Do you set unrealistic expectations on yourself?

Have you ever said to yourself that you're going to try and do it all? Whether it's changing your job, losing 10 pounds, running a half marathon, writing a book, volunteering and... whatever it might be. And, all at the same time?! Or perhaps it's one big thing like losing weight. But your plan is to cut out sugar, wheat, dairy, caffeine and alcohol, and exercise every day, and all this from a place of having not done much exercise and eating what you want, when you want.

I totally have. There was a time when I wanted to start my own business, lose a certain amount of weight by following a strict paleo diet, start a supper club, write a book, fall in love, and I wanted it all to happen within the next month.

Throughout a lot of my adult life I've gone through phases like this – where if I was going to do something, I had to do it all at once or there wasn't any point in doing it. I believed it was purely down to sheer willpower and I just had to keep strong, stick to my 'perfect' plan, and everything would happen according to how I wanted.

Now, I am all for having dreams and goals and setting the bar high for what you want in life – I truly do believe that anything is possible. But, looking back at my plans for how I wanted to achieve these things, I have tended to be a bit unrealistic in my expectations on myself.

It's natural as humans to want change to happen overnight. We live in a society which favours things moving at lightning speed and if anything takes too long, we're not interested any more. We also think that all it takes is a 'can do' attitude and 'to do' list the size of your arm, to get anything done. But often we don't take into consideration that life is stressful and busy and that we are human, yes, we are human! We have 'on' days and 'off' days and can't always predict what might come up. Also, if we are trying to live from one extreme to another and expecting a lot, we are naturally going to get tired and possibly burned out leading to the opposite of what we want happening.

Slowing down and dealing with one thing at a time rather than having these high expectations and radical changes to implement is so much more manageable and hence achievable! Less really is more.

Where do you set unrealistic expectations on yourself?

47.   How do you talk to yourself?

One day I was going through some of my childhood things, which had been stored at home in Kenya, to sort out what I wanted to keep and what I was ready to let go of.

It was quite an emotional thing to do; looking through old photos, report cards, letters, ornaments, finding my sticker books, toys I once had and adored, even my old diaries from my teens – which was quite an eye-opening experience.

There was the usual teenage talk about which boy at school I was in love with, which seemed to change on an almost weekly basis! But what left me feeling sad was the way I spoke to myself. There were pages about how much I disliked my body and wanted it to be something else. Loads on how much I didn't want to be me. Some of this can be attributed to teenage hormones and angst I'm sure, but I also realise how this negative self-talk paved the way for so much of my teens and twenties. I was on a constant journey to lose weight, battling with my natural body shape and size. I was never happy with myself and compared myself to others frequently. Everything I did came from a place of unhappiness, thinking that if I changed who I fundamentally was, then I would be happy.

As I've shared, this was reflected in the way I treated myself. What we say to ourselves really does shape the way we live on a daily basis.

Throughout my twenties I'd pinch my belly and look at my dimply thighs, telling myself how disgusting they were. I'd get frustrated with myself if I couldn't wear a certain size of clothing or if I hadn't lost any weight within a couple of days of following a controlled diet. I'd tell myself I have to do better. I'd feel guilt and shame for food and alcohol binges and tell myself I was weak and that I had no will power.

Over time I've consciously and slowly changed the way I speak to myself and would be ashamed to talk the way I did to anyone else or even out loud to myself.

Rather than focusing on the negative I congratulate myself for the good and try to see the positive in any situation.

I try to be kinder and more compassionate and talk to myself as someone I care about and only want to give the best to. It was hard at first and I had to pretend I was someone I cared about initially, but it got easier over time.

Have you ever stopped to notice what you tell yourself on a daily basis? What thoughts run through your head when you are looking in the mirror. When you perhaps get something 'wrong'? Can you talk to yourself in the same way you would someone you love?

48. Developing a kind relationship with all parts of yourself.

While today I have a much happier, healthy relationship with myself compared with when I was in my teens and twenties, there are of course still days when I want to revert to old habits or feel like I want to hide under the duvet with every season of a show I want to watch.

What I've learned and am still learning to do, is not be so hard on the parts of me I don't like so much. The parts of me that perhaps hold me back and want to fall into old patterns of self-sabotage. The parts which choose to be lazy and skip the workout and order a take-out. The parts which aren't the 'perfect' person I thought I once needed to be.

Stopping and thinking what I'd say to a best friend in the same situation has meant I'm kinder and more understanding. This has helped me to bounce back from these moments into a place where I feel back in my flow a lot quicker; whereas in the past I'd feel guilty and spiral into self-loathing if I did something I wasn't 'proud' of, which could last for a few days and sometimes weeks.

I also did the below exercise in my book writing mastermind, which I am now sharing as it was truly powerful in helping me to accept all parts of myself.

Starting with the words I am... write down everything that comes to mind.

I am a creator

I am compassionate

I am a being of light

I am nice

I am impatient

I am a coach

I am fast

I am a quick-thinker

I am generous

I am loving

I am bored at times

I am lazy

I am a procrastinator

I am selfish

I am un-lovable

I am self-centred

I am worthy

I am lovable

I am deep

I am dark

I am a bitch

I am a healer

I am self-abusive

I am hurt

I am broken

I am joy

I am wonder

I am amazement

I am beauty

I am love

I am magic

I am addicted

I am shadow

I am a self-sabotager

I am attention seeking

I am mean

I am judgmental

I am caring

I am evil

I am unkind

I am self-serving

I am alone

I am beautiful

I am the Universe

I am me

I am a witch

I am all I can be

I am good and bad

I am abundance

I am free

Declaring and owning everything 'I am' out in the open was a bit of a realisation, incredibly healing as well as an affirmation that it's okay to be all of it. Even if I am all the parts that I am not so proud of, I'm also all the parts I am proud of.

Your turn, what are you? How does it feel to declare all of it?

What parts of yourself do you perhaps not like so much but could show some more compassion and understanding to?

49. Forgiveness

Forgiveness has the power to heal.

What are you holding on to from your past that you can forgive? Perhaps an argument that was never resolved, or a situation where you felt wronged. In your mind (or out loud, or in a journal if you prefer) forgive the person/people involved and wish them well. This doesn't mean you have to be the best of friends now or even have them in your life, but simply forgiving and letting go so you can find peace within.

Or, it may be time to forgive yourself for something and move on?

Who or what is it time to forgive in your life?

A letter to my dad

Dear Dad

We've never really spoken about what happened. I don't think we ever needed to. There was just this knowing that all was now different, and we could move past everything that had happened.

I'll be honest, it's taken me longer than I thought it did to fully move on and heal. I thought everything was fine, but there'll still be moments of sadness, moments of anger, pain and frustration, which can be triggered by the weirdest things.

Growing up, before mum died, I remember how close we were. I loved coming on jogs with you, you'd always keep a watchful eye on me and encourage me when I swam length after length in our little pool, coming into your darkroom was a treat for me – getting to see all your photographs and how they came to life in a bowl full of chemicals. You were such a fun dad, and I always felt protected and safe when you were there.

I was so lost, sad and confused when that all changed. When you didn't know how to be a parent anymore. When you lost control, I began to despise you. To resent you. To hate being around you. You made me so angry. So disappointed.

I know now that you were doing your best and you were in pain too. It was just so hard for me to understand at the time. I thought I'd totally lost you for a while back there. I used to pretend you weren't around anymore as I truly didn't think you'd ever be you again. I am so glad that you came back to you though. So glad you turned things around and admitted your weaknesses and pain. So glad you took the steps to heal with the support you needed. Since then you've done nothing but inspire me and I am so glad to have you back, dad.

I know that we have all been through a lot and I honestly can say I am truly grateful, for everything, today. I know you are sorry for some of the things that happened, and I forgive you for 'disappearing' for a while.

50.   Ho'oponopono

As part of my own healing journey, I've spent a lot of time working on forgiving and loving myself more. One day after meditating, I found myself wanting to write a letter to my body – an apology for all I've done to it.

The letter, in itself, was incredibly healing, but I also realised later that it followed the steps of Ho'oponopono, an ancient Hawai'ian practice for forgiveness, without me even consciously doing it.

Ho'oponopono is a simple yet powerful practice – all you have to do is think of something you want to forgive and let go of and really imagine it, feeling it fully. Then repeat the following four phrases:

I'm sorry
Please forgive me
Thank you
I love you

These phrases can be used in any order, feel free to change them around if that works better for you. Then keep repeating them as you think about the experience etc, really feeling the words as you say them.

As you say the words, it can be helpful to think of the following:

'I'm sorry' – I acknowledge the situation and am sorry for it.

'Please forgive me' – I release it from myself, no longer allowing it to affect me.

'Thank you' – thank you for all you have taught me.

'I love you' – I send love to the situation/person etc.

Doing this may bring up some emotions (in my experience it always has). Hopefully it will bring you to a place of feeling what needs to be released and/or allowing it to be.

I first came across Ho'oponopono in a workshop and I had a huge emotional release as I really connected with the things I wanted to forgive and let go of. Writing this letter was such a cathartic experience for me, as I really connected, felt true gratitude, sorrow, remorse and then love for myself. Here is the letter I wrote.

A letter to my body

Dear body,

I want to say I'm sorry for the way I've treated you.

I've said horrible, even abusive things to you. I've hit you; I've drowned you in alcohol and numbed you in drugs.

I've stuffed you so full you couldn't move, then I forced you to purge to release the fullness.

I allowed men to invade you in an effort to feel connection and wanted, but I often felt empty afterwards as I was so disconnected from you, I didn't feel those things. The only thing I felt was disgust, shame and hatred.

I'd bury you in baggy clothes not wanting you to be seen.

I tried to change you in any way possible, I wanted to alter you, make you appear different – in colour...shape...size – anything ... so you weren't YOU.

The only thing I wanted was for you to be different.

I am so sorry. I am so sorry. I am so sorry.

Please forgive me for the years of abuse. Please forgive me for treating you as separate to me. Please forgive me for my neglect. I acknowledge you and all that you have done for me.

You've held all my pain and sadness. You've carried me when I felt alone. You've allowed me to see the beauty on this planet. You've enabled me to feel love and compassion towards others. You've shed tears when I needed release. You've been there for me every day of my life.

Thank you for being there for me always. Thank you for being so resilient. Thank you for holding me on my journey.

I love your silky, brown softness. I love your curves and little dimples. I love that you are a bit wonky in places. I love that you carry the stories of all my experiences. I love that you are me. I love that I am me. I love that we are me.

I will continue to be kind to you. I promise to prioritise your wellness. I will make time for rest and movement and I will honour what you have to say. I will surrender into your wisdom and knowing.

This is my promise to you. From now on it's us together.

I love you body, Love me.

51.   Learning to trust myself

This was hard in the beginning for me as I had such low self-confidence and felt all over the place.

Also, in society we are literally told how to eat, what we like, what's good for us, when we should be getting married, when we should have children, what job to do. We are literally programmed NOT to make our own decisions. Or at least not ones that go against the status quo.

I've always known inside that I didn't want to do life the way everyone else was doing it, the way society dictated. But believing that it was okay, and that I wasn't mad for wanting different things from what everyone else seemed to want, took some time.

As I gradually began to look for others who had followed their dreams, I saw more and more examples of how people had gone against the norm, trusted themselves and followed their intuition.

I began working with an amazing mentor who helped me with some fun tools to begin trusting myself. The first was the 'yes' 'no' game. Where I would ask my body to show me what a 'yes' was, then what a 'no' was. For me it felt like my body contracted for a no and felt spacious for a yes. I would then ask a simple yes or no answer question and pay attention to how my body felt. I began practicing with this and it was amazing. I got the answer, and when I acted on it things had a way of turning out in my favour. Every time.

This was so cool; it was like I had discovered a magic tool that had been there all the time. As I played with it, I actually started to 'hear' the answer to the question I was asking and began to ask questions like 'Which bus should I take?' – the answer came, and I'd get on that bus and have the smoothest bus journey with a seat! This, if you live in or have visited London, you'll know is not generally the norm.

As I continued to do this, I strengthened this 'trust muscle', and now I feel the answer almost before I even ask the question!

Do you trust yourself? What can you do to strengthen this trust?

52.   Self-compassion

Truly beginning to care for myself was the turning point in me beginning to feel like me.

As I peeled away the layers that I had built up around myself, I uncovered the pain and feelings that had been buried and never felt.

I allowed myself to mourn the death of my mother, I empathised with myself for feeling like I had to figure it all out on my own.

I forgave myself for all the pain I'd self-inflicted, and acknowledged that I had coped in the way I knew best.

I no longer cared about questions to do with my identity. I'm proud to have such a diverse background and love that I can identify with people and places all over the world. I want to learn more about my Indian heritage and embrace it as a part of me. In fact, that's where I feel the next part of my journey will take me.

I started to like myself and put myself first, which radically changed my life as my outer world began to reflect how I was feeling inside.

This self-care journey has not been one straight line. It's been a few years of trialling new things, feeling good at times, then being messy and not feeling so good. It's generally headed in a positive direction but is by no means 'perfect', or maybe it is perfect, as I'm exactly where I need to be.

Today, above all I feel happy that I have found my way back into my body, I have found my way back to ME.

Where in your life can you give yourself more self-compassion?

Next Steps

If you would like to continue your self-care journey as a sensitive being, I have a number of resources that may support you – in the workplace and in general.

I have a free **Facebook group – Self-care for empaths**, which you can join here: http://bit.ly/empathselfcare.

I offer **free 30-day seasonal (in the northern hemisphere) self-care challenges**, in April, June, September and November, where you will receive a daily self-care tip, action or inspiration straight to your inbox. You can find out more and join here: http://bit.ly/30daysofselfcare.

I have a **monthly membership group – Seasonal self-care for sensitive souls**. It's a space to dive deeper into your self-care allowing it to flow with the changes in weather as well as honouring your cyclical nature:
http://bit.ly/sensitive-souls-self-care

If you would like to **explore your inner cyclical nature more**, here is a free PDF chart you can download to track your menstrual cycle alongside the moon cycle: http://bit.ly/mooncyclechart.

Finally, please also check out my website **www.tarajackson. co.uk,** to keep up to date with my ongoing self-care journey and where I am at today, as well as how I can support you, other free resources, offers and where we can connect on social media.

Acknowledgements

I am beyond grateful to everyone that has been a part of my journey so far.

I would like to say a HUGE thank you to all of the incredible people who have helped me with writing this book and bringing it into the world, which in itself has been an incredibly healing and transformational experience.

Nicola and my awesome mastermind ladies, without this mastermind I'm not sure I'd ever have started writing this book! Thank you for the wonderful space you created and held Nicola, which allowed me to write in the way I wanted, not that I felt I 'should'.

Thank you Anna for reading an early draft and giving me such helpful feedback.

Thank you David for always believing in me and encouraging me to write when I was procrastinating!

Julia, I am so grateful to you for holding space for me to go through all the feelings I re-went through as I wrote it. Long live our WhatsApp voice clips!

Lara, Cathy, Kasia, Gwen, Sara, Meron, Janneke, Dominique, Moriah and all my Circle sisters – thank you ladies for helping me with ALL the resistance that came up while I was writing, for giving me healing sessions to help me through some of the harder emotions, and for helping to keep me accountable. I am so lucky to have you all in my life!

Thank you Maya, Michelle, Nik, Lele, Lulu, Dee, Alice, Harshita and dad for reading the early drafts and for giving me such helpful and encouraging feedback. Thank you especially Lele for helping with the final bits when I was so ready for it to be done.

Louise, thank you so much for letting me use the cottage as such a peaceful and inspiring place to write outside of London.

Thank you to all the people who are in my group 'Self-care for empaths' and on my mailing list, I am grateful to have you and have learned so much from being able to share with you all over the past two years.

Finally, a MASSIVE thanks to all of the incredible people (family, friends, even people I don't know) who supported me with my GoFundMe and pre-orders to self-publish this book. I am blown away by your generosity and kindness. Thank you, thank you, thank you for helping me to make this possible.